HORRIBLE SCIENCE

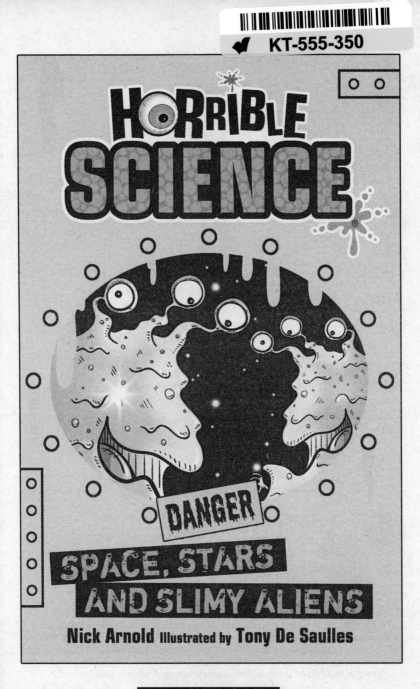

DANGER

SPACE, STARS AND SLIMY ALIENS

Nick Arnold Illustrated by **Tony De Saulles**

■SCHOLASTIC

www.horrible-science.co.uk

Scholastic Children's Books,
Euston House, 24 Eversholt Street,
London NW1 1DB, UK

A division of Scholastic Ltd
London ~ New York ~ Toronto ~ Sydney ~ Auckland
Mexico City ~ New Delhi ~ Hong Kong

First published in the UK by Scholastic Ltd, 2003
Abridged edition first published by Scholastic Ltd, 2014
This edition published 2018

Text © Nick Arnold, 2003, 2014, 2018
Illustrations © Tony De Saulles, 2003, 2014
Index by Caroline Hamilton

ISBN 978 1407 18542 2

Printed and bound by CPI Group (UK) Ltd, Croydon, CR0 4YY

2 4 6 8 10 9 7 5 3 1

The right of Nick Arnold and Tony De Saulles to be identified as the author
and illustrator of this work respectively has been asserted by them in accordance
with the Copyright, Designs and Patents Act, 1988.

Paper used by Scholastic Children's Books are made from wood grown in sustainable forests.

CONTENTS

Nick Arnold has been writing stories and books since he was a youngster, but never dreamt he'd find fame writing about outer space. His research involved staring at stars and trying to burp in space. He applied to be an astronaut but got turned down for telling terrible jokes.

When he's not delving into Horrible Science he spends his spare time eating pizza and riding his bike (but not at the same time).

www.nickarnold-website.com

Tony De Saulles picked up his crayons when he was still in nappies and has been doodling ever since. He takes Horrible Science very seriously and even agreed to jump into a black hole. Fortunately, he's made a full recovery. When he's not out with his sketchpad, Tony likes to write poetry and play squash, though he hasn't written any poetry about squash yet.

www.tonydesaulles.co.uk

INTRODUCTION

THE STAR FIGHTER TRIED TO ESCAPE...

STEP ON IT!

OOER!

BUT THE ALIENS WERE CLOSING IN!

ERK!

Space movies are great, aren't they? Don't you just love the speeding spacecraft, perishing planets and slobbering aliens? And isn't it a pity when some tedious teacher says, "Oh, but it's all made-up"? But what they don't tell you is that real-life outer space is even more scary than the scariest space movie!

In a moment, we'll blast into space to boldly go where no science book has gone before. Our mission is to find out why space is so scary. And why just going for a walk in space without your spacesuit can boil your spit, burst your lungs and give you the worst sunburn ever.

Then, if we survive outer space, we'll be peering at putrid planets and sizzling stars and mad moons. Horrible places, the lot of them. And we'll be finding out fearsome, foul and funny facts such as…

• How the Sun *sings*.

• Why you shouldn't burp in space.

• Which stars turn you into slime.

• Why your body bits are made of blown-up stars.

Yes, these and many more facts really are true … er, hold on … our space expert, Luke Upwards, wants to say something…

Oh all right! Scientists aren't sure if aliens exist. And if you must know, I made up the alien story in this book. Mind you – we will be looking at our chances of meeting real-life aliens.

But the rest is really real – even if it sounds like it's off on another planet. And hopefully you'll feel that space is an out-of-this-world subject and you'll be encouraged to find out more. And who knows? Maybe one day you'll become an astronaut and live your own true-life space adventures.

So who needs movies? Just grab your popcorn and settle down in your seat. The show is about to begin!

SPLATTERING SPACE

Earth is a small blue ball floating in a big black sea. And the big black sea is as dark and dangerous as a bad-tempered black bear in a coal cellar! Later on we'll find out how deadly dangerous space really is — but first it's time to check out the basic background bits.

So what's floating about up there?

Space, stars and slimy aliens fact file

Name: Stuff in space

The basic facts: Here are the main things that you might see in space...

1 Stars – balls of super-hot gas like the Sun that blast heat and light (see page 25 for the sizzling details). Nearly all stars are hugely bigger than planets but in 2005 scientists found a pathetically weedy star not much bigger than Jupiter.

2 Galaxies – swirling whirls of billions of stars.

3 Planets and dwarf planets – big spinning balls of rock and gas that orbit (whizz round a star). One orbit is a year and one spin is a day. Dwarf planets such as Ceres, Pluto and Eris are smaller than planets.

4 Solar System – the Sun and planets that orbit it.

5 Moons – rocky objects that orbit planets and dwarf planets.

6 Asteroids – large space rocks that orbit the Sun. Most of them hang out in an area called the Asteroid Belt. (The details are on page 128.)

7 Comets – balls of ice and rock that orbit the Sun on the edge of the Solar System. Some comets fly close to the Sun. (For more details, why not steer your spacecraft to page 181.)

Slimy secrets: Some stars aren't lucky stars if you go too near them. These twinkling terrors could cook you to a puddle of slime. (If you're interested and feeling really brave you can turn to page 30 for the dangerous details.)

But there's more to space than planets and galaxies — a whole universe in fact. Fortunately, there's a way to squeeze the whole universe into three minutes...

WELCOME TO THE THREE-MINUTE UNIVERSE TOUR...

Get ready to switch on your imagination because you're going to do more imagining than you've ever imagined before. We're going on a three-minute tour of time and space. Don't forget to put on your spacesuit and set your watch to Planet Splott time...

ERK!

WARNING! YOU'D BEST PUT ON A CRASH HELMET BEFORE READING THIS NEXT BIT!

First stop: the Big Bang

It's 13.7 billion years ago and the universe has popped out of nothing. It started as a tiny point of heat and energy but in less than one second it's bigger than a galaxy. In the first 20 minutes many of the atoms that make up you formed in the brain-boggling heat. Maybe it's a bit too hot – let's get out of here!

Second stop: quaking quasars

It's ten billion years ago and the universe is much bigger – it never stopped growing. The first galaxies have formed and early stars are more violent than a bear in a honey shop. Black holes have formed in the centre of the new galaxies and they rip matter apart as it whirls towards destruction. Some horribly hungry holes can gobble 1,000 stars in a year and blast energy two trillion times brighter than the Sun. Astronomers call these blasts quasars. Hmm – maybe this isn't a good spot for a picnic.

Third stop: the Milky Way

We're floating in space billions of kilometres from our own galaxy – the Milky Way. Isn't it lovely? Aha! That's Earth down there.

If you're on Earth and a long way from streetlights, the

Milky Way looks like milky drool dribbled across the night sky by a giant baby... Except it's not milk. It's stars. About 200,000 billion stars, in fact. And they're bunched together because you're seeing them from the side (look at a dish and you'll get the idea).

The Milky Way is just one of over 40 galaxies called 'the local group'. And the local group is one of 400 galaxy groups known as the Local Supercluster (but that's not as local as your local supermarket). You might like to know that we're in an interesting-sounding gas cloud called the 'local fluff' which is part of an area known as the 'local bubble'.

Fourth stop: Earth

In 1990, scientists launched the Hubble Space Telescope to see the stars from space and they tried peering at a speck of sky the size of a stick-insect's eyeball on the end of your out-stretched fingertip... You might think they found one measly star. But they found more ... much, much more.

THE DAILY SOLAR SYSTEM
15 January 1996

WOTTA LOTTA SPACE!

Scientists are stunned by the latest findings from the Hubble Space Telescope.

Even in a tiny bit of sky there are 2,000 galaxies. Earth-based telescopes can see billions of stars, but clouds and dusty air can spoil the view. The Hubble Space Telescope has a much clearer view from outside the Earth's atmosphere. Said one awe-struck astronomer, "It makes me feel very small and spaced-out!" She then disappeared into a darkened room with a cup of tea and a headache pill.

Two thousand galaxies could mean 200,000 BILLION stars and those were just the galaxies Hubble could make out… But the amazing truth is that scientists reckon that space is nearly all empty, er, space. If the universe was 30 km wide and 30 km high, all the stars and galaxies and planets and slime ice cream from Planet Splott would scrunch into an itsy-bitsy grain of sand.

Fifth stop: the universe in one million billion years time

It's dark. It's cold even by space standards because most of the stars have spluttered out. Even the longest-lived stars eventually burn out or get sucked into black holes. There is scarcely any energy around for living things to consume. The trouble is that energy is always being lost as heat and now the universe is too big and matter is too scattered for gravity to pull together new stars. Eventually even the black holes will disappear. It's all very sad and dreary – scientists have even got a nice cheerful name for how the universe will end – heat death. Maybe it's time to go home for a nice hot drink.

THE MIND-BLOWING MYSTERIOUS UNIVERSE

Having toured the universe in three minutes you might think that astronomers know it all – but they don't. Here are some maddening mysteries to mull over…

Where has 96 per cent of the universe got to?

According to scientists, the stars and planets, etc. that we can see should only amount to 4 per cent of the universe. The other 96 per cent seems to be hiding. The experts think that 22 per cent of the universe could be objects such as black holes that we can't see or detect but where's the rest got to? Some boffins reckon there could be undiscovered particles out there – all very mysterious.

Why is the universe growing so fast?

In the 1990s, scientists were shocked to find that the universe wasn't behaving itself. It was growing too fast to fit their theories. According to the experts this is due to a mysterious power called dark energy that pushes things apart. It would be handy if they were right since dark energy could be the missing 74 per cent matter of the universe … and yes, you did read that right because you can actually make matter from energy.

Why aren't we over-run with aliens?

There could be one billion planets in the Milky Way like Earth. So why aren't slimy aliens crawling out of our plugholes? Well, they might be too distant to contact us. I mean, the universe is many trillions of kilometres across and we can't send them our address and expect a postcard…

Earth
The Solar System
Orion arm
(that's one of the swirling sticking out bits)
The Milky Way
The Local Group
The Local Supercluster
The Universe
OOPS! Sorry I've forgotten the postcode.

Dear Earthlings

Found you at last! Must pop round for tea sometime!

Love the Aliens XXX

17

A radio or light signal would be quicker. They whizz along at 300,000 km per second or 9.46 million million km per year – I guess they're so fast because they're travelling light. Scientists call this distance a 'light year'. But the Milky Way is 100,000 light years across and a chat with aliens could take 10,000 years. And I bet your phone bills would be ASTRONOMICAL.

Mind you, that hasn't put off some scientists. A series of SETI projects (SETI = Search for Extra-Terrestrial Intelligence) searched for alien radio signals but so far without result. Maybe aliens aren't smart enough to build radios? Or maybe they don't want to know us?

What's that? You want to go looking for aliens … and dark matter and dark energy and you can't wait to leap into your spacesuit and go and see space?

Not so fast! You don't think you'd be allowed to whizz off in a multi-billion dollar spacecraft just like that, do you? You need *years* of training before you're allowed near one of those things. But while you're waiting for your training to start, you can always read our super sci-fi space story. And guess what? The first episode shows what space is *really* like…

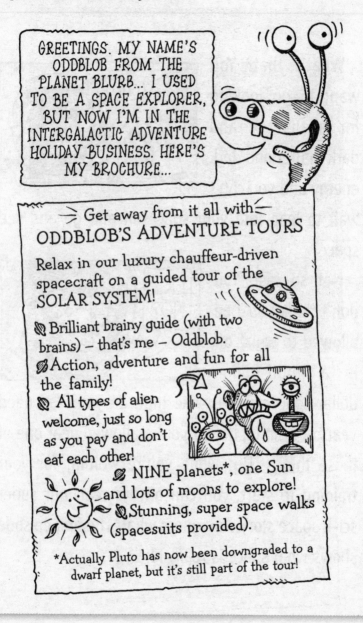

GREETINGS. MY NAME'S ODDBLOB FROM THE PLANET BLURB... I USED TO BE A SPACE EXPLORER, BUT NOW I'M IN THE INTERGALACTIC ADVENTURE HOLIDAY BUSINESS. HERE'S MY BROCHURE...

⇒ Get away from it all with ⇐

ODDBLOB'S ADVENTURE TOURS

Relax in our luxury chauffeur-driven spacecraft on a guided tour of the SOLAR SYSTEM!

🐌 Brilliant brainy guide (with two brains) – that's me – Oddblob.

🐌 Action, adventure and fun for all the family!

🐌 All types of alien welcome, just so long as you pay and don't eat each other!

🐌 NINE planets*, one Sun and lots of moons to explore!

🐌 Stunning, super space walks (spacesuits provided).

*Actually Pluto has now been downgraded to a dwarf planet, but it's still part of the tour!

The small print

1 Oddblob will warn you about the dangers of each planet you visit. So you mustn't blame him if you get killed.

2 If you leave the spacecraft, you must remember to put on a spacesuit. If you forget you'll spend your final seconds wishing you had a better memory.

IMPORTANT SCIENCE NOTE

Hmm – sounds like Oddblob's spacecraft is faster than anything known on Earth. Our human spacecraft would take years to travel between the planets. For example, the unmanned Voyager 2 craft was launched in 1977 and didn't get to Neptune until 1989 – that's 12 years later!

My story begins when I took a booking from a family of aliens. They wanted to tour the Solar System, but they were a bit messy... They even left alien dribble on my brochure.

Here's the alien family. Slobslime is a Snotty from the Planet Splott. And she's not the smartest alien in the universe.

And here's her baby, Sloppy. She lives in an egg-pod, but in 100 years time she'll hatch into an adult Snotty like Slobslime.

On the first day of the aliens' holiday I tried to get them used to living in space.

Things went wrong from the start. Our first outing was a walk in space, but Slobslime had forgotten some vital equipment...

ARE WE READY?

YOU BET! I COULD DO WITH SOME FRESH AIR!

YOU'VE FORGOTTEN YOUR SPACESUIT!

Seconds later, Slobslime suffered the effects of being in space without a spacesuit.

Space can be colder than -100°C. That's cold enough to freeze skin solid. Sunlight can be hotter than 120°C, hot enough to burn the skin to a crisp. Slobslime was frozen like a slime-lolly on one side and roasted to a slime-crisp on the other.

With no air to press on Slobslime's body from the outside, the air in her body pushed outwards. Soon her twelve lungs were about to pop. Without air pressure her tears and slimy green spit began to boil like gloopy green soup.

Deadly rays, known as radiation (ray-de-ay-shun), from the Sun blasted Slobslime. Soon she'd be cooked from the inside like a Blurbi-turkey in a microwave. With seconds to spare I pulled Slobslime to safety and, after a few hours of body repairs in my spacecraft's sick bay, she was back to her old slimy self.

ANOTHER IMPORTANT SCIENCE NOTE

It looks like Snotties have incredible powers of healing and recovery. Any human who did this would certainly be killed!

So you see, there are loads of dangers in space – but at least the stars look great. As the Hubble Space Telescope showed, you get a lovely clear view. Mind you, there are ways to see stars without risking a roasting in space. You could bang your head (but that's not too clever).Or you could point your telescope at the next chapter.

STAGGERING STARS

It's easy to stare at the stars but it's not so easy to explain them. You might even come up with some curious questions...

HOW ARE STARS MADE?

HOW DO STARS WORK?

ARE THEY ALL THE SAME?

OK, OK – here are some answers. Let's start at the beginning (it's better than starting at the end). How are stars made? Well, I know a great way to find out how stars are made. Let's ask our very own local star – otherwise known as 'the Sun'. I bet he'll tell us how he works, too...

THE SUN'S SECRET STORY

by our reporter Randall Scandal

He's definitely the biggest star in our Solar System – a legend in his own lifetime. When I met the Sun, he was in a sunny mood in his exclusive home in the centre of the Solar System. For a big 4.6-billion-year-old ball of hydrogen gas, he didn't look at all bad.

Randall: How did you become such a big star?
Sun: I remember it like it was yesterday. Though it wasn't yesterday – it was 4.6 billion years ago.

Randall: So how did it all begin?
Sun: At the time I was nothing. Just a big cloud of dust and gas floating around in space. I was a bit of a drifter.
Randall: But you pulled yourself together?
Sun: You bet I did!

I'm not too sure what happened since I wasn't feeling too bright at the time but I figure some superstar blew up and gave me a nudge. Anyhow I started pulling gas and dust into a ball. I was having a ball when I got my act together and landed my STARRING role!
Randall: So what happened?

Sun: As I got bigger, I got hotter – that's when I really shone!

Randall: So what was the secret of your success as a star? What really makes you tick?

Sun: Well, I guess if you're a star, you must have what it takes…

Randall: What's that?

Sun: Enough gravity to crush your hydrogen gas into a substance called helium. Star quality – that's what I call it!

Randall: And that gives you energy?

Sun: Some of the hydrogen gets turned into heat and light energy. It certainly keeps me going!

Randall: But in the early days, success didn't come easy – it took a few million years before you became a star.

Sun: Yeah, it was hard work!

Randall: And meanwhile your planets were forming…

Sun: Yeah – that was the outer part of my cloud. They're part of my dazzling success.

Randall: I know, I've got sunburn.

Well, the Sun's got a good memory! The Earth and the other planets really did start off as bits of dust and gas. The bits pulled together to form small rocks. And the small rocks clumped into bigger rocks and then mini-planets. The mini-planets smashed together and the bits joined up to form the planets as they are today.

Now for the question that I bet you're asking at this very second. What was doing all this pulling and smashing of dust and gas and rocks to make stars and solar systems? Without it, we wouldn't be here, so I guess it's a matter of some gravity. Hey, that's the answer – it's a force called gravity!

GREEDY, GRASPING GRAVITY

Gravity is vital for getting a handle on space and everything in it and you've got to know about it to make sense of the rest of this book. But it's a bit *scientific*.

ARGH! NOT AGAIN!

WARNING – SCIENCE FACTS COMING UP!

Space, stars and slimy aliens fact file

Name: Gravity

1 All matter pulls on other matter – we call this pulling force 'gravity'. Its energy is carried by gravitational waves. Scientists detected them in 2017.

2 The force pulls on everything else as it reaches across space.

3 The Earth's gravity pulls you towards it and your gravity pulls the Earth towards YOU!

4 As you go further from Earth, gravity gets weaker. But gravity still works billions of kilometres away. That's why the Sun's gravity stops the planets zooming off into space.

Slimy secrets: The bigger and heavier you are, the stronger your gravity is. That's why the Earth (being bigger than you) pulls you down towards it when you jump. Possibly with painful results...

So that's the nitty-gritty of gravity. But I nearly forgot the final question from page 25 – are all stars the same? No – they're not ... and their ultimate fate depends on how big they are...

BET YOU NEVER KNEW!

Stars more than 12 times smaller than our Sun are too small to work. This kind of 'failed star' is called a brown dwarf. (It's not to be confused with one of Snow White's little helpers in a bad mood. That's a browned-off dwarf.)

Meanwhile big stars, roughly ten times the size of the Sun, have some horrible heavyweight habits…

SINISTER SUPER-STARS' SECRETS

Big stars are bad news. Would you believe it – before they're even *born* these murderous mega-stars in the making are already causing chaos in the cosmos! Stars of all sizes form in huge clouds of dust and gas (as in the Sun's story on page 26). But as a big star takes shape, it zaps smaller wannabe stars with gas and blasts them to bits.

30

Big stars are greedy gas guzzlers, too. They make more heat and crush hydrogen into helium faster than smaller stars like the Sun. And, after 11 million years, the star crashes inwards – pulled by the force of its own gravity!

The centre bounces out again ... only to hit the outer part of the star which is still falling in!

The BIG BASH bursts the star to bits in a blast brighter than ONE HUNDRED BILLION stars! It's called a supernova and it's a real super-star show-stopper. And that, you might think, is that… After all, the sinister super-star is blown to itsy-witsy bits. Or is it?

You know those horror films where the monster is supposed to be dead but suddenly comes back to life? Well, it happens in real life with big stars…

After the blast, the centre of a star carries on shrinking. But it doesn't die – it turns into a scary mini-monster known as a neutron star.

It's just 20 km across. And you might think that's too small to be dangerous. But here's what happens if you get too close to it…

The neutron star is incredibly heavy. This gives it GIGANTIC gravity. If you landed on a neutron star, the gravity would make your body so heavy that a tiny flake of dried snot would weigh ONE MILLION TONNES. This could make a very large hole in your hankie.

YOUR HOUSE ON EARTH

B'DOING!

YOUR SNOT ON A NEUTRON STAR!

SPLURP!

Would you fancy a neutron-star holiday?

Horrible Holidays present...

The Neutron Star Hotel

Check into our out-of-this-world ONE-STAR hotel...

WELCOME!

GASP!

Unique atmosphere! It's so heavy that it's only 2.5 cm high. At least you can enjoy an all-day lie-in as you struggle to breathe!

Work-out in our exclusive gym. Just lifting your head uses more energy than climbing Mount Everest.

URRRRRGH!

You'll want to come back as soon as possible. And even if you don't – the gravity will pull you back!

Some neutron stars are known as pulsars. They spin so fast that the whole star can turn 360 degrees in less than a second. And they blast out beams of radio waves like whirling flashing space sirens.

But there is one type of neutron star that makes that seem rather relaxing. I'm talking about the mean, murderous magnetar.

The magnetar is like a giant magnet – but you wouldn't want one on your fridge. Imagine a very stupid astronaut decides to visit a magnetar. When he gets to within 400,000 km the magnetism drags his metal spacecraft to its doom. When he's 1,000 km away the fatal force zaps his atoms and turns him into slimy soup by pulling them out of shape. Not a nice way to go.

But really big stars – those weighing more than 20 Suns – turn into something *even more nasty*.

Something that makes the mean magnetar look warm and fluffy. With these really big stars, the bit left after the supernova blast shrinks into … A HORRIBLE BLACK HOLE! Visiting a black hole could spoil your 'hole' day – but if you wanna try it…

Horrible Holidays present…

The Black Hole Hotel

Why not 'drop-in' for a 'hole' lot of fun?! It's more than just a hole, it's a hole in the universe. And you'll find its pull hard to resist! Once inside, you'll enjoy a quick break! Well, several breaks, as your body is pulled into long stringy bits and squished smaller than a pinhead and never seen again… You'll be thrilled to bits…

YES, VERY LITTLE BITS!

Oh, so you don't fancy spending your holidays in a hole? And you'd rather clean a toilet with your toothbrush… Oh well, cheer up!

THERE'S A STAR IN EVERY BODY!

You see, those exploding giant stars aren't all bad news. Bet you never knew that much of your body is made of bits of blown-up stars! Here's your very own incredible insides story…

Like every other star, giant stars spend time happily crunching hydrogen into helium. But not always. When the giant star is overheating and about to go pop, it crushes more and more bits of matter together and starts churning out other substances. The oxygen in your lungs, the iron in your blood and the carbon in your body were all made by an exploding star billions of years before you were born.

And now, at long last, it's your chance to have stars in your eyes. Yes, folks – it's star-staring time!

THE HORRIBLE SCIENCE STAGGERING STARGAZERS' CLUB

Every night sees the most eye-popping show in the universe. It's called the stars and here's your chance to join a brainy band of star-spotters who are setting out to explore the universe using their eyeballs. Welcome to the Staggering Stargazers' Club!

Stuff needed for stargazing

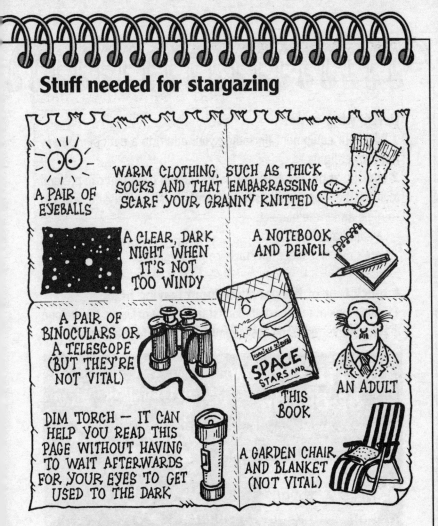

A PAIR OF EYEBALLS

WARM CLOTHING, SUCH AS THICK SOCKS AND THAT EMBARRASSING SCARF YOUR GRANNY KNITTED

A CLEAR, DARK NIGHT WHEN IT'S NOT TOO WINDY

A NOTEBOOK AND PENCIL

A PAIR OF BINOCULARS OR A TELESCOPE (BUT THEY'RE NOT VITAL)

SPACE STARS AND — THIS BOOK

AN ADULT

DIM TORCH — IT CAN HELP YOU READ THIS PAGE WITHOUT HAVING TO WAIT AFTERWARDS FOR YOUR EYES TO GET USED TO THE DARK

A GARDEN CHAIR AND BLANKET (NOT VITAL)

IMPORTANT NOTE

Don't leave home without your adult. Also, do remember that adults get scared easily so don't wander off and leave them!

Here's what to do...

1 Take your equipment (including your adult) to a dark place away from street lights.

2 Look up at the sky. If you sit in the garden chair you can pretend to sunbathe – or should I say 'star-bathe'? If you feel cold, you can snuggle under the blanket.

Got all that? Great!

Here's our first space spectacle coming right up!

A quick tour of the galaxy without leaving home

1 Take a look at the constellation (star pattern) of Orion. It's the one that looks like this. (The best time to see it is after Christmas.)

CONSTELLATION OF ORION

BETELGEUSE

DO YOU NEED A TORCH?

ORION NEBULA

SIRIUS

RIGEL

2 Can you see Sirius – the brightest star in the sky? It's about 8.6 light years away from us and 23 times brighter than the Sun. The only reason why you're not screaming,"AARGGGGH! MY EYEBALLS!" is that Sirius is so far away that we only see a tiny bit of its light.

3 Now back to Orion… Did you know that stars can be different colours? Cooler stars can be red and hotter stars are bluish-white. Most star colours are too faint to see clearly, but you can see some in Orion if you look carefully:

- Rigel is a giant, hot, blue-white star up to 900 light years away and 40,000 times brighter than the Sun.
- Betelgeuse is at least 600 times bigger than the Sun and thousands of times brighter. Luckily for us it's over 420 light years away. It's a 'red supergiant' star – you might be able to make out its tasteful orangey-colour. It's a kind of gruesome glimpse into the future of our Sun at the end of its life when it'll swell up and fry the Earth to a frazzle. (See page 194 for the red-hot details.)
- The Orion Nebula looks like a little twinkling cloud – you'll only see it if the sky's really dark. It's over 1,300 light years away and is part of a bigger, darker cloud that's 100 light years across. It's a sort of nursery where cute little baby stars are born – you can even see the baby stars twinkling. Who's a pretty baby then?

Note to readers in the southern half of the Earth

Orion can be seen from all over Earth except for the South Pole. But in countries south of the Equator, it'll appear upside down compared to how it's shown on page 40. So you could put the map upside down. Or if you want to do things the hard way you could stand on your head to stare at the stars! And instead of looking for Sirius, you might like to check out Canopus. It's here:

This giant star is 12,000 times brighter than the Sun and so far away its light takes 300 years to reach us. And that's a long way to come for a flying visit. So long! Have FUN!

But we're not. You see we're heading for the most important star of all. It's the star at the centre of our Solar System and the star we all depend on for light and heat. And if you 'tan' the page, you'll find that the next chapter is a red-hot read!

THE STUNNING SUN

The Sun is an ordinary, yellow star like millions more in the Milky Way. But it's still powerful and stunning. And the stunning Sun's sunshine is incredibly important for all of us on Earth...

SIX STUNNING SUN STATISTICS

1 The Sun is so hot that a pinhead heated in its centre would give off enough heat to kill a person 160 km away.

2 Imagine an iceberg 2.5 metres thick. The Sun's hot enough to melt the ice in 2 hours and 12 minutes, even though the iceberg is 150 million km from the Sun.

But just think... The Sun blasts heat in all directions all the time.

So imagine that you built a wall of ice 2.5 metres thick around the Sun at a distance of 150 million km.

Even though your wall would be 949 MILLION km long – the Sun could melt it *all* whilst you're enjoying a nice film. SCORCHING!

3 Every second, the sizzling Sun guzzles 564 million tonnes of its hydrogen fuel. I bet its gas bills are gigantic! Every minute, 235 million tonnes of hydrogen turn into energy. That's equal to ONE MILLION elephants blowing up every second! SENSATIONAL!

4 The Sun (and the Solar System, including us) are spinning around the centre of the Milky Way at something like 230 km a second. Reckon that sounds fast? It is. But it still takes 225 million years to do one lap – called a cosmic year. So far, the Sun's managed 20 laps – so it's 20 cosmic years old. STAGGERING!

46

5 The Sun 'sings'. Yes – *really*! The Sun's surface wobbles in and out. Waves of wobbling pass over the Sun's surface like the waves of air called sound waves. Sadly we can't hear the Sun's song. There's no air to carry the sound and, anyway, it's too deep for our Earthling ears to hear. But scientists have used a computer to make a similar sound and then made the sound higher-pitched so we can hear it. It's a deep rumbling noise – like a hungry hippo with a grumbling tum. SURPRISING!

6 The Sun gives off radio waves. They're just another form of radiation, like light or X-rays. Maybe the singing Sun could cut a single and play it on its own radio station? SHATTERING!

But the most stunning Sun fact of all is that without the Sun's heat and light, it would be night all over Earth for ever. It would soon start to get very cold and all the plants would die. And then all the animals that live off plants would die, too, and we humans would have nothing to eat. It doesn't bear thinking about – as any bear will tell you…

But despite the fact that the Sun is so obvious and important, we can't look at it…

Hmm – the Sun sounds a bit dangerous. But the aliens in our space sci-fi story are flying towards the sizzling Sun. Will they end up cooked?

Oddblob's Alien Adventure

We set off for the boring, yellow star known as the Sun. I told the Snotties that we wouldn't get too close to the star. If we did, our flying saucer would turn into a frying saucer, *snirk snirk**. Instead, my plan was to keep a safe distance and switch on our light filters so that we wouldn't get blinded.

On the way to the Sun, Sloppy became bored...

I had to explain that the Sun is easy to see because it's large and bright (unlike Sloppy who is neither large nor bright). But as any super-intelligent Blurb knows, it's a long way away. Afterwards,

* Ha ha! in Oddblob's language.

Sloppy played a game of snotball with my pet robot Blurbi-dog, Roverbot.

BLURBI-DATA

BY COSMO THE COMPUTER

- ☼ NAME: The Sun
- ☼ SIZE: Diameter 1,392,000 km*
- ☼ SIZE COMPARED TO EARTH: One million times larger
- ☼ GRAVITY COMPARED TO EARTH: 28 times stronger
- ☼ LENGTH OF DAY: Like a planet, the Sun spins in space but takes 28 Earth days to turn round once
- ☼ ATMOSPHERE: Super-heated gas called the Corona. Steer clear of it - it's 2 million$^{\circ}$C

*Diameter = distance side to side across its centre.

☀ WEATHER FORECAST: It's going to be UNBEARABLY HOT. The Sun's surface is about 6,000°C and its centre is 15 million°C! It's also going to be windy – but the wind isn't made of air. It's bits of atoms blasted from the Sun. There's also lots of deadly radiation.

☀ TRAVEL TIPS: Keep your distance. But if you must go close, wear super-thick Blurbi-shades and sunscreen and make sure your spacecraft has a really thick heat shield.

As we hovered at a safe distance, I pointed out the most interesting sights.

- Bumpy bits – the surface of the Sun looks like a sweet Earth fruit called an orange. The bumps are the tips of rising currents of hot gas.

- Sunspots – those simple-minded Snotties reckoned the Sun had snotty-pox spots! I told them they were sunspots – dark spots on the surface made by magnetic forces. They are 1,500°C cooler than the Sun's surface but still blistering hot!

- Solar flares – these are a bit like a Snotty's slimy sneeze only the snot is bits of hydrogen. They can reach Earth and knock out primitive Earthling electrical equipment. That's the flares, not the Snotties' sneezes, snirk, snirk.

WARNING BY COSMO!

Solar flares are hot enough to bake a Blurb. If my sensors spot one, I'll warn you. But beware - the flares zoom at 400 km a second. So you'd better move fast, Oddblob!

From 20 million km away, Cosmo's super-sensitive sensors scanned the Sun's insides…

BLURBI X-RAY OF THE SUN

CHROMOSPHERE

PHOTOSPHERE

CONVECTIVE ZONE

RADIATIVE ZONE

CORE

SWEAT!

CHROMOSPHERE - This is the inner atmosphere. It's 10,000 km deep.

PHOTOSPHERE - This is the surface of the Sun. It's 300 km deep.

CONVECTIVE ZONE - This is the area where hot gases rise up from the core. It's 200,000 km deep.

RADIATIVE ZONE - 380,000 km thick.

CORE - 380,000 km across. Heat energy is made here.

It was too hot to go any closer to the Sun, but we did enjoy a Blurbi-barbecue.

Now for a fascinating fact… The Sun makes up 99.86 per cent of all the matter in our Solar System. It doesn't sound much, but the teeny leftover 0.14 per cent includes the most incredibly interesting bits of the Solar System … the planets!

And right now we're about to tour the Solar System. We'll voyage from melting Mercury to perishing Pluto and explore the weird worlds in-between. Just climb aboard…

AND DON'T FORGET YOUR TOOTHBRUSH!

HOT AND HORRIBLE PLANETS

Anyone stupid enough to mess about on Mercury or visit Venus has less chance of escaping than a balloon in a pin factory. These planets are so hot and horrible that they would turn a person into goo in a fiery flash. You wouldn't send your worst enemy there … would you?

HERE WE GOO…

A suffering scientist has been sent to Mercury by her worst enemy. She soon discovers that the planet moves in a weird way with an eerie effect on the days…

MY TRIP TO MERCURY by Ivana Coldrink
(sorry about the scorch marks)
I arrived on Mercury this morning just in time to watch the Sun rise. It climbed in the sky and as it climbed it seemed to get bigger.

Around noon, I was about to eat my sandwiches when I noticed that the Sun had started to move backwards. I was so surprised that I forgot to eat, and my sandwiches turned into burned toast.

A little later, the Sun changed its mind and went forwards again. At the end of a very long day, it set in the evening but now it's reappeared! Suffering space rocks! What's going on?

Oh well, Ivana – you've got to suffer for science and this science sounds seriously scintillating. Here's what's happening…

So what's up with the Sun?

As Mercury orbits the Sun, it travels in a shape called an ellipse. It looks like this…

When Mercury is closer to the Sun – the Sun looks bigger. When the planet moves away from the Sun – the Sun looks smaller. And because a day on Mercury lasts 59 Earth days – and that's most of a Mercury orbit (88 Earth days) – the Sun can change size during one day. With me so far? Great! Now for the backwards bit…

On Earth, the Sun appears to cross the sky every day as the planet spins in space. But just imagine if our planet were spinning a lot slower. Well, then the Sun would seem to move slower. And if our orbit were faster than the speed the Sun seemed to move, the Sun would appear to go backwards. That's what happens with the slowly spinning Mercury! See what I mean?

Hmm – Mercury sounds mad. Oh well, let's catch up with our space story and see if Oddblob can make sense of mixed-up Mercury...

Oddblob's Alien Adventure

We set off for Mercury. It's the closest planet to the Sun – a quick hop of about 58 million kilometres.

BLURBI-DATA

- NAME: Mercury
- SIZE: Diameter 4,879 km
- SIZE COMPARED TO EARTH: Three times smaller across
- GRAVITY COMPARED TO EARTH: A little over one-third. That means you would be one-third your Earth weight, Oddblob.
- MOONS: None
- LENGTH OF DAY: 58 Earth days and 12 hours
- LENGTH OF YEAR: 88 Earth days
- ATMOSPHERE: Hardly any
- WEATHER FORECAST: Too hot AND too cold. During the day it's 427^0C - that's hot enough to melt a tin of Blurbi baked beans. And there's no escape from the Sun's radiation. At night, it's -183^0C.
- TRAVEL TIPS: It's not a sensible place to go - but if you really must visit Mercury, you'll need your spacesuit, your Blurbi-shades and extra-thick thermal socks for those long cold nights.

As we swooped over Mercury, I pointed out the main tourist attractions. This didn't take very long as there aren't many.
• Cliffs – 3 km high.
• The Caloris Basin – a crater 1,550 km across.
• The deep craters have ice in them.

The Snotties pestered me to let them go skating in the craters. But I decided to move on 50 million km to Venus. I hoped it would be more interesting. And it was, but not in a nice way…

BLURBI-DATA

NAME: Venus

SIZE: Diameter 12,104 km

SIZE COMPARED TO EARTH: A bit smaller

GRAVITY COMPARED TO EARTH: A little weaker

MOONS: None

LENGTH OF DAY: 243 Earth days

LENGTH OF YEAR : 225 Earth days. No, Oddblob I am not blowing my Blurbi-chips! The planet spins so slowly that one Venus day lasts longer than one Venus year! And just to confuse you a bit more Venus spins backwards compared to all the other planets...

ATMOSPHERE: Choking clouds of carbon-dioxide gas. The atmosphere is heavy enough to crush you flat and the clouds are full of acid that could dissolve what's left of you.

Then there are the volcanoes ... they're not erupting at present - but they might start at any moment.

◐ WEATHER FORECAST: Today's going to be hot, 500°C to be exact, just the same as every day. It's the hottest place in the Solar System (not counting the Sun).

◐ TRAVEL TIPS: I'd rather crash my computer chips than go to Venus!

Despite Cosmo's advice, I decided to land, even if we stayed in the spacecraft. But the Snotties wanted to go outside…

At this point Roverbot decided to go walkies…

This gave me the chance to point out the dangers of…

After I'd rescued Roverbot with the spacecraft's robot arm, he seemed rather upset and took it out on me…

But if Venus the planet is vicious and violent, Venus the god was vile! The Mayan people of Central America thought the planet was a god (not a goddess as the ancient Greeks believed). And Mayan priests spent lots of time looking at the planet to see what their god was up to. Was he moving? What time of day did he appear?

COULD YOU BE A MAYAN ASTRONOMER?

This quiz is based on real events. It's the year 562. You're the priest-astronomer to King Sky-witness of Calakmul. But are you an awesome astronomer or a feeble fortune-teller?

1 It's 29 April. You know that on
this day Venus will appear to stand
still in the sky. What do you tell
the king?
a) It's a good day to bash your
enemies.
b) It's a good day to do a bit of
shopping.
c) It's a bad day — you'd best go to
bed and hide under the duvet.

2 The king's army captures the rival
city of Tikal with its king, Double
Bird. What do you do with him?
a) Lock him in a small room and make
him do hard sums.
b) Agree with him that life is very
unfair and let him go.
c) Crush him under a wheel-shaped
rock and cut his heart out.

3 Also captured was a royal prince named Animal Skull. He's only a boy. What do you do with him?

a) Drown him in a pot of custard. Then eat the custard.

b) Make him king and excuse him from going to school.

c) Tikal, I mean tickle him to death with a feather duster.

4 What do you do with King Double Bird's army?

a) Treat them to a slap-up supper.

b) Pull out their fingernails and cut out their hearts.

c) Send them to work in the royal chocolate factory.

ANSWERS

1a) To the Mayans, the god Venus was in charge of war and disaster. If he's hanging about in the sky (as seen from Earth) it's a good time to ask for his aid.

2c) He was a sacrifice – a little thank-you prezzie for Venus.

3b) But the boy has to do what you tell him to.

4b) Venus likes sacrifices – he's a real 'hearty' character.

If you really want to be a Mayan astronomer, here's your chance to view Venus with your own eyes. (Just leave the stone knives at home!)

THE HORRIBLE SCIENCE STAGGERING STARGAZERS' CLUB

Don't forget the things you need from page 39!

Viewing Venus

Here's what to do…

1 Look out for Venus in the west, two hours after sunset. (You should be able to see the planet for about half the year – so if it's not there it'll turn up in a few months.)

2 Venus looks like a brilliant bright star. It's so bright because the Sun's light reflects off the planet's deadly choking clouds. Isn't that pretty?

Did you find Venus easily? Hopefully you did. But, in the past, viewing Venus has presented plenty of puzzling problems. It even wrecked some astronomers' lives.

This is the story of poor Guillaume Le Gentil. In 1761, this French scientist was keen to see a transit of Venus. That's when the planet moves across the face of the Sun as seen from Earth. With me so far?

For astronomers, a transit is something special. It's the chance of a lifetime to measure how big and far away Venus is compared to the Sun. A transit was due in 1761 and the best place to see it was India – so Guillaume sailed off to India. But his plans flopped faster than a bungee-jumping hippopotamus. If Guillaume had sent his scientific buddies letters they might have sounded like this (complete with a dodgy French accent)…

1761 (In India)
To ze French Academy of Sciences
Bonjour, guys!

I hev some good news and some bad news. Ze good news is that I hev seen ze transit and ze weather was sunny so I saw everything. Zoot allors! Eet was gobsmacking! Ze bad news is that owing to ze war with Britain I couldn't land – so I 'ad to watch ze transit from my ship and I couldn't set up my scientific equipment.

DARN!
DARN!
DARN!
DRAT!

Ze weather is terrible. It eez pouring with rain but I hev decided to stay in India to wait for ze next transit. It's not due for another eight years but at least I'll be in ze right place zees time!
Au revoir!
Guillaume

PS Zere is green mould growing on my wig.

After seven years of waiting, Le Gentil did some calculations. To his dismay, he found that he'd get a better view from Marianas Island in the Pacific

Ocean. So he set off for the island as soon as he could. But, once again, his luck was out...

1769

I em'ere

Bonjour, guys! .....
Darn! Darn! Darn! I em in manila in ze Philippine Islands and I hev just found out zat I hev meesed ze only ship zat goes to Marianas Island. I asked when ze next one goes and it won't be for another THREE years!

Oh well, mustn't grumble, as ze British say. I reckon I weel still get a good view of ze transit from 'ere.

Au revoir!
Guillaume

PS Ze bugs hev eaten a huge hole in ze backside of my trousers.

But the Academy had other ideas. They decided that Le Gentil would get a better view back in India. So he was sent back the way he had come – with fateful results…

1769

Bonjour, guys!
Darn! Drat! Curses and FRILLY KNICKERS! I sailed to ze India like you told me to. I got zere in time. I set up my telescope. I was so excited I couldn't sleep. I'd been waiting EIGHT long years for zees! Ze next day ze Sun was shining. I was all ready for ze transit and then… ze sky clouded over and I did nat see a thing! And now I hev just 'eard zat in Manila where I wanted to stay zere was a blue sky and everyone saw the transit. And the next transit isn't due for another 100 years! ARRGGGH! I em jumping up and down on my mouldy wig!

Yours crossly

Le Gentil

_1770_

Bonjour, guys!

You do remember me – don't you? Eez me – Guillaume and I'm home! I hed a terrible voyage back from India. Well, it was three voyages actually – I kept getting shipwrecked. My trousers are all cut to pieces and my wig is washed overboard.

Well, when I got 'ome, everyone thought I was dead and my 'orrible family were just dividing up all my belongings.

Au revoir

Guillaume

PS My family says I should thank my lucky stars I em still alive. Grr – don't mention ze stars or planets or I will scream –ARGH!

Oh dear… Well, you'll have no trouble seeing this next planet. You probably see it every day and you might well be an expert on it! Yes, it's time to get down to Earth!

DOWN TO EARTH!

If I were an alien looking for somewhere to live, I'd certainly choose Earth. After all, it's the only planet with running water, air and the chance of finding a decent pizza. But enough of me – it's time for another episode of our slimy space story. Let's find out what the aliens think of Earth…

Oddblob's Alien Adventure

Earth would be a perfect planet to live on if it weren't overrun by those annoying half-witted humans. Mind you, when we landed on Earth, the Snotties acted almost as half-wittedly as the humans…

BLURBI-DATA

🌍 NAME: Earth

🌍 SIZE: Diameter 12,756 km

🌍 MOONS: One — the Moon

🌍 LENGTH OF DAY: 24 Earth hours

🌍 LENGTH OF YEAR: 365.25 Earth days

🌍 ATMOSPHERE: 78% nitrogen, 21% oxygen. The rest is other gases including 0.038% carbon dioxide (increasing with human pollution).

🌍 WEATHER FORECAST: It's going to be hot around the Earth's middle and well below freezing at the poles (each end). A large amount of water will fall from the sky in the form of small drops. Earthlings call this rain.

🌍 TRAVEL TIPS: Human scientists have invented a portable roof. This item of equipment is carried in the hand and protects the head from rain. It's called an Um-brell-a. It's worth taking one of these with you if you go out. Some life forms on Earth are extremely unfriendly and fierce and might try to eat you.

BEWARE OF

SHARK

TIGER

CROCODILE

As we approached Earth, I pointed out a couple of interesting features...

- Earth is mostly blue because of its water – 71 per cent of the planet is covered in masses of water known as seas. Even the clouds are made of tiny drops of water floating in the air. As usual, those half-witted humans have got it wrong – they should be calling their planet Water rather than Earth or maybe Planet Damp and Drippy, snirk, snirk.

- Earth teems with life. You can see it from space – for example, huge areas of land are covered in giant green life forms known as trees. Despite their size, trees do not appear to be dangerous and have never been known to chase anyone.

Slobslime and Sloppy had never seen Earth's life forms and they hadn't been listening to my talk on trees...

Then Slobslime met her first human.

The human had a dangerously fierce Earth creature with her…

On Earth, there are billions of tiny life forms called microbes – these can cause disease. Slobslime seemed to have fallen ill.

Well, I think Earth's lovely. OK, so I'm biased, but everyone who sees Earth from space is amazed at how pretty the planet looks with its shiny blue seas and its fluffy white clouds. Earth reflects so much sunlight it seems to glow in the dark...

Here's what astronaut Jim Lovell said back in 1968:

The vast loneliness up here is awe-inspiring, and it makes you realize just what you have back on Earth. The Earth from here is a grand oasis in the big vastness of space.

Earth's ultimate secret

Apart from its beauty, you might not think that Earth's that special. Of all the planets in our Solar System, it's the third hottest planet with the fifth-fastest spin. It's the fifth heaviest planet and it has

77

the fourth-strongest gravity. So what makes the Earth so special?

Notice anything?

Earth's in the middle of every list! Being the Solar System's Mr Average is what makes Earth special! It means that Earth isn't too hot or too cold for life. And it means that Earth's gravity is just right for all the life forms that live on it.

Including you and me.

But it doesn't stop there. Earth has other fantastic features that make it safe for life. My shady pal, Honest Bob, has moved into the second-hand planet business and he's keen to sell you the Earth. Can you spot what's wrong with his advert?

We'll be back after this commercial break…

78

HONEST·BOB'S USED·PLANETS

"Honest Bob is as honest as the day is long but I wouldn't want to meet him after dark." – Bob's mum.

THE EARTH

Built-in security features...

• The Earth is like a giant magnet. Yes, it makes a magnetic force.

MAGNET

MAGNETIC FORCE

• The magnetic force blocks harmful radiation from the Sun in the Van Allen belts.

So why not take the Earth for a test spin? It's yours for only £10,000,000,000.25 – so guess what? It ain't gonna cost the Earth!

So would you buy the Earth off Honest Bob? Hope not! As far as I know, the Earth isn't actually for sale! Let's ask Luke Upwards about the rest of Honest Bob's claims…

Honest Bob was right about the Earth's defences against the Sun. But what's this? It looks like Izzie Starrs who works with Luke has a joke she wants to share with us…

BET YOU NEVER KNEW!
The Van Allen belts, named after US scientist James Van Allen who found them in 1958, are between 1,000 and 60,000 km from Earth. The Sun's radiation gets trapped by the Earth's magnetic field in the belts. But if a spacecraft broke down there, the astronauts would be revoltingly roasted by the radiation.

Now let's take Honest Bob up on his offer to take the Earth for a spin. We can because…

Shock horror news! Earth is moving!

Right now, you're whizzing through space at about 30 km a second (that's about 108,000 km an hour) as Earth whizzes around the Sun. In fact you've actually whizzed 300 km since the start of this sentence. And what's more, you, me, the cat and the goldfish and the entire Earth are *spinning,* too!

HOW TO ENJOY A FREE ROUND-THE-WORLD TRIP WITHOUT GETTING OUT OF BED

All you have to do is stay in bed all day at a point on the equator (the imaginary line around the Earth's middle). As the Earth spins in space you'll move with it. In one day, you'll travel a distance equal to going around the world. That's right — you enjoy a free 40,000-km space ride at 1,670 km an hour, *without getting out of bed!*

Now let's imagine you pushed your bed to the North Pole (or the South Pole if you prefer sleeping upside down. Just make sure that duvet's really thick!) While you stay in bed all day, your bed will go around in a little circle like an ice skater in a tight spin. Confused? Hopefully this will help:

If you're at the North Pole, you can look up and see the Pole Star directly above your head. All the other stars seem to go around it in a circle as the Earth spins in space. Of course – you don't have to go to the North Pole to see the Pole Star. Anywhere in the northern half of the Earth will do…

THE HORRIBLE SCIENCE STAGGERING STARGAZERS' CLUB

First collect the things you need from page 39!

Peer at the Pole Star

Here's what you have to do...

1 Head for a dark place away from street lights.

2 Look up at the sky. Find the constellation called the Big Dipper or the Plough. The lovely romantic star names in the Plough are Arabian.

CONSTELLATION OF THE BIG DIPPER

DUBHE
ALCOR
MIZAR
MEGREZ
ALIOTH
ALKAID
MERAK
PHEKDA

HOW ROMANTIC!

LOOKS LIKE A SAUCEPAN, TO ME!

Follow the line from Merak to Dubhe upwards and you're peering at the Pole Star.

3 Can you see Alcor? It helps if it's a dark night! A thousand years ago the Arabs reckoned that you had good eyesight if you could spot Alcor.

4 The Pole Star is a giant star 2,000 times brighter than the Sun but, as luck would have it, it's a nice safe 480 light years away.

5 Since the star always appears directly over the North Pole — you can always tell which direction is north, even at night!

BET YOU NEVER KNEW!

Earth's spin has an embarrassing wobble. And that means by the year 14,000 the North Pole will be pointing to a different star. DRAT – this book will be out of date! But after another 12,000 years, we'll be pointing at the Pole Star again and you can blow the dust off this book and read it again!

Hold on – if you live in the southern half of the Earth you may be a bit miffed because you can't see the Pole Star. Don't be cross – you can stare at the Southern Cross instead!

THE HORRIBLE SCIENCE STAGGERING STARGAZERS' CLUB

Check out the Southern Cross

1 Here's where to look for it…

CONSTELLATION OF THE SOUTHERN CROSS

GAMMA CRUCIS

JEWEL BOX

COAL SACK

ALPHA CRUCIS

IS THAT STARDUST?

NO, IT'S COAL DUST!

2 If the long arm of the cross were five times longer, it would end up above the South Pole.

3 Now here's a shock (I don't think). The Coal Sack is nothing to do with dirty lumps of coal and you won't find jewels in the Jewel Box. The Coal Sack is a big, dark cloud of gas and the Jewel Box is a group of distant stars.

Mind you, it doesn't matter where you live in the world – there's one thing in space everyone can see. Yes – you'd better turn that page fast or we'll miss our flight to the Moon!

THE MADDENING MOON

The Moon's story started four billion years ago when the Earth got hammered on the head by a small planet and the weather changed. And here's the whole head-banging history...

THE BIG BASH

When Earth was whacked by a Mars-sized planet, the big bash blasted red-hot rocks into space. Gravity grabbed the rocks and rolled them into a ball and – BINGO! – the Moon was made. And that's how the seasons started too.

You see, Earth was knocked off balance and ever since it's been leaning over at an interesting angle of 23.44 degrees.

So when the Earth goes round the Sun, the northern and southern halves of the planet take it in turns to lean towards the Sun and have summer. And now we've got the seasons sorted, it's time for another instalment of our slimy sci-fi story...

Oddblob's Alien Adventure

As we neared the Moon, I asked Cosmo the computer for some info on the place. But first I had to clean the green slime off his computer chips. Grrr – those slobbering slime-slopping Snotties!

BLURBI-DATA

NAME: The Moon

SIZE: Diameter 3,474 km

SIZE COMPARED TO EARTH: A quarter its width

GRAVITY COMPARED TO EARTH: One sixth

LENGTH OF DAY: Nearly 28 Earth days

LENGTH OF YEAR: 365 Earth days and 6 Earth hours

ATMOSPHERE: Nothing much...

WEATHER FORECAST: The weather's going to be either too hot or too cold. During the day it's 120°C and blasted by radiation from the Sun. At night, it's -170°C. But at least there'll be no rain because there's no water, and no wind because there's no air.

TRAVEL TIPS: Wear spacesuits and leave the umbrella in the spacecraft.

From space we had a great view of the Moon and I showed the Snotties the most interesting sights.

- Craters – the Moon's craters were made by crashing exploding space rocks. There are over 300,000 craters and those slug-brained Snotties tried to count them all. Some craters are thousands of metres deep and their bottoms never see the Sun. Some of them contain ice.

- The Earth – when you're on the Moon, the Earth looks much bigger and brighter than the Moon does when seen from Earth. This is because the Earth is bigger than the Moon.

- The 'seas' – sadly, these are silly Earthling names for masses of dark rock that melted when giant space rocks hit the Moon 3.8 billion Earth years ago. No chance of space surfing, I'm afraid!

Baby Sloppy heard me say "seas" and thought we were going to the seaside…

Because the Moon is smaller than the Earth, the gravity is weaker. This means that everything weighs one-sixth of its Earth weight. This came as a surprise to the Snotties…

Hmm – the Moon sounds cool! Sadly, NASA won't let me go into space because my terrible jokes might mess up the mission. Oh well, it's almost as much fun to stare at the Moon from Earth. Fancy a staring match?

THE HORRIBLE SCIENCE STAGGERING STARGAZERS' CLUB

Make eyes at the Moon
Things to look for…

1 What shape is it?
Possible shapes

CRESCENT   FULL   GIBBOUS

IMPORTANT SCIENCE NOTE
The shapes depend on the angle the Sun is shining on the Moon as it orbits the Earth. The new Moon appears as a skinny sliver so close to the Sun that it's hard to make out. And it grows into a big round Moon before shrinking back into a crescent.

2 What time is it?
The new Moon rises at sunrise and sets at sunset. When the Moon is waning (getting thinner) it rises at midnight and sets at midday.

The full Moon rises about sunset and sets about sunrise. So the higher the full Moon is in the sky, the later it is.

3 Can you see any details?
Here are three things you can spot without a telescope…

Note to readers in South America, Australia, New Zealand and southern Africa

You'll see the Moon like this:

No matter where you are on Earth, you'll only ever see one side of the Moon. And no, it's not because the Moon doesn't want us to see the other side… It's because the Moon only turns once as it circles the Earth. To show how this works, Luke Upwards is sitting in my swivel chair as Izzie Starrs walks around him. Luke's pretending to be the Earth and Izzie's the Moon. Hey – you might like to try this at home too!

BACK OF IZZY'S HEAD IS THE FAR SIDE OF THE MOON!

TOP VIEW OF LUKE

IZZY TURNS ONLY ONCE AS SHE CIRCLES LUKE. HE NEVER SEES THE BACK OF HER HEAD!

Like the Moon, Izzie makes one turn each time she goes around Luke. Hmm – in that time Luke ought to make 28 of the turns we call 'days'. I'll just whizz him round. OH YUCK! Luke's been space-sick!

Well, by now you may be feeling you've mastered some of the Moon's maddening mysteries. But does that make you an awesome astronomer? Or are you simply spaced-out? Find out with these cosmic quizzes...

COSMIC QUIZ 1

Mad Moon scientists have come up with some incredibly idiotic ideas about the Moon. Which idea did I make up?

1 William Pickering (1858–1938) and George Darwin (1845–1912): The Moon was thrown off the Earth as it spun in space billions of years ago. The hole left by the Moon is the Pacific Ocean.

2 Frédéric Petit (1810–1865): There are TWO moons, the second one is very small.

PEAR-SHAPED? HE MUST HAVE BEEN BANANAS!

3 Peter Hansen (1795–1874): The Moon is pear-shaped.

4 Hans Hörbiger (1860–1931): The mountains on the Moon are made of ice. There have been lots of moons, but they crashed to Earth and wiped out the giants who lived there.

ANSWERS

1 TRUE. And they weren't too wrong – as you'll remember from page 88.

2 TRUE. In the 1850s a lot of annoyed astronomers got eye-strain searching for the second moon. No one's found it yet.

3 FALSE. Wrong! Ha ha! As if the Moon was pear-shaped! NO – Peter Hansen said the Moon was egg-shaped and the end that we can't see is covered in jungle. So there!

4 TRUE. He must have been as barking mad as a dog up a tree! Maybe that's why nasty Nazi leader Adolf Hitler hailed half-crazed Hans as the world's greatest scientist.

You might think that these theories were as daft as the man who ate the skin and threw away the banana. And, of course, you'd be right – but could *you* do any better?

COSMIC QUIZ 2

Which two items have been found
on the Moon?
a) Germs that normally live up
your nose.
b) Dust that
smells of garlic.
c) Multicoloured
bits of glass.
d) Slimy green
lettuce.

ANSWERS
a) Yes. OK, so germs don't live on
the Moon but these germs were
found hiding in a camera in 1969.
The camera had been taken to the
Moon by an earlier spacecraft. The
germs had been sneezed there when
the camera was loaded on Earth and
they were none the worse for their
holiday on the Moon.
b) No. Moon dust smells of
gunpowder not garlic.
c) Yes. Most Moon dust is black and
shiny — which is why the Moon
appears to shine brightly. But Moon
dust also contains tiny bits of

coloured glass made from melted
minerals.
d) No. But plants grow well in
Moon dust (with added water and
air). So who knows? One day we
might see gardening programmes
from the Moon featuring lunar
lilies and crater chrysanthemums.

WHAT'S IN A NAME?

The first scientist to peer at the Moon through a
telescope, Italian super-scientist Galileo Galilei
(1564–1642), thought the Moon had 'seas'. And
he even gave these places names…

Seas that you might like to visit on the Moon…

• The Bay of Rainbows

• The Lake of Dreams

Seas that you might want to avoid…

• The Ocean of Storms

• The Marsh of Decay

• The Lake of Death

THE PUZZLING PLACE- NAMES TORTURE TEST...

Certain places on the Moon and the planets are named after places and people from Earth. This is handy for staggering a scientist.

Questions to ask...

1 ARE THE ALPS IN EUROPE?

"Yes," they say – quite rightly, since the Alps *are* in Europe. You say, "No, they're on the Moon!" This is also true, since the Alps *are* mountains on the Moon.

2 WHERE IS ARABIA?

ER...

If they say, "It's in the Middle East", you can say, "No, it's a desert on Mars." This is just as true. And now the quiz gets crueller...

You can say, "Not the famous composer – I mean the 643-km-wide crater." Mercury's craters are named after famous arty people and that's why Mark Twain and Leonardo da Vinci *are* on Mercury. Just to confuse your victim, you could add that Beethoven is also an asteroid.

Many Moon craters were named by Italian astronomer Giovanni Riccioli (1598–1671). Riccioli christened craters after famous astronomers. The crafty crater-namer gave himself and his scientist pal, Grimaldi, generously giant craters but he didn't like Galileo so he gave him a crumbling cruddy crater...

GRR — I RATE A GREATER CRATER!

Mind you, even the chilly dark side of the Moon is cosy and cheerful compared to our next stop. Living on this planet must be as jolly as a blocked drain. And is it really the home of monsters – or is that just an ugly rumour?

MONSTERS ON MARS?

Mars is the must-see planet for monster hunters. In this chapter, you'll stumble across monster scenery, monster stories and who knows what else? You might even find a few microscopic Mars monsters squirming and slithering over the next few pages…

Yes, there's something about Mars that really wakes folk up – it's even been known to work on people who haven't woken up for years. In 1997, people all over Earth watched a live TV broadcast from Mars on the Internet. No, they weren't glued to an alien TV station – a camera on the Sojourner space probe sent pictures that were transmitted on the Internet.

Actually, the live show was more of a dead show. Nothing appeared to happen on Mars and there was nothing to see except hundreds of rocks and a pretty pink sky. There would have been more life in a graveyard at midnight but, even so, one billion people gazed at the scene in awestruck amazement.

The really exciting part of the mission was when a man named Brian Cooper used virtual-reality software to drive a radio-controlled robot car named Rocky about on MARS! Would you like a Rocky for Christmas?

See you after the commercial break.

HONEST BOB PRODUCTS PROUDLY PRESENTS...

FANCY A DRIVE ON MARS?

It's an out-of-this-world experience!

Built-in chemical test kit for rocks!

"RUMBLE!"

For just £99,999,999.99 you can own this lovely little Mars rover!

Real whizzy top speed of 1.4 km per hour – WOW!!!

Virtual-reality kit and software to control it from your own computer!

THE SMALL PRINT - 1. Mars has millions of rocks with silly names like *Yogi* and *Scooby Doo*. If you smash into a rock, you might break your toy. It takes 15 minutes for your radio signals to reach Mars, so you'd better plan where you're driving!
2. If your car falls over, you'll have to send your mum or dad to Mars to put it upright.
3. The battery only lasts 90 days – and that's if you're lucky!

Oh well, it was fun while it lasted. Sadly, I've just heard that spoil-sport NASA scientists won't let me drive a robot car on Mars. But if that's got you interested in visiting the planet, I guess you've got a choice...

a) You could hang about waiting for a manned flight – there'll be one in a few years and, who knows, they might let you come along for the ride. OR

b) You could try this experiment now and get an idea of what to expect on Mars...

DARE YOU DISCOVER ... HOW TO CAUSE A MARTIAN DUST STORM?

You will need:

TORCH

BALLOON

TALCUM POWDER

A TABLE

AN UNDERSTANDING FAMILY

What you do:

1 Darken the room or wait until dark. Switch on the torch and place it so that it shines on the table from the side.

2 Sprinkle the table with talcum powder.

3 Blow up the balloon and let out the air a few times.

4 Now blow up the balloon and place the mouth of the balloon so that the escaping air blows over the top of the table.

You should notice:

The dust swirls out in a big cloud, billows into the air and floats about like a 100 per cent genuine Martian dust storm. Great, isn't it? In fact, just like on Mars, the dust storm starts when the wind blows bits of dust against each other that knock into more dust, etc.

WARNING TO
YOUNGER READERS

Ask permission before blanketing your home in a talcum-powder dust storm. If you don't, you might be sent to Mars, or possibly to your bedroom, until the dust settles!

And now it's time for another slimy slice of sci-fi story action. This time the aliens explore Mars…

Oddblob's Alien Adventure

Mars is my most favourite planet in the Solar System! The scenery is massively more magnificent than Earth and there are no half-witted humans to spoil the view! I decided to show the Snotties the delights of mountaineering on Mars. And I asked Cosmo for the background basics…

BLURBI-DATA

NAME: Mars

SIZE: Diameter 6,792 km

SIZE COMPARED TO EARTH: Half Earth's diameter

GRAVITY COMPARED TO EARTH: Not much more than one third as much

MOONS: Deimos and Phobos -- they're only a few km across

LENGTH OF DAY: 24 Earth hours and 37 Earth minutes

LENGTH OF YEAR: 687 Earth days

ATMOSPHERE: Just a few wisps of carbon dioxide

WEATHER FORECAST: It's going to be very cold (about -55°C) but at least it won't rain. After all, it hasn't rained for four billion years. There's a chance of a dust storm that could last days. Don't worry, Oddblob — the winds are weak because there's so little air. It won't be windy enough to blow you away.

TRAVEL TIPS: Soil chemicals can dissolve your space boots and some of your 24 toes.

As we came in to land on Mars, I showed the Snotties the superb scenery…

GET A LOAD OF THIS LOT…

- The Mariner Valleys are amongst the Solar System's vastest valleys. They're 7 km deep and 240 km wide – that's four times deeper and eight times wider than that crack in the Earth known as the "Grand Canyon". And at more than 4,000 km long, that's almost enough to stretch across the puny Earthling country known as the United States of America.

- There are river valleys and lakes where water flowed on Mars billions of years ago. Some rivers were more than 24 km wide and 100 metres deep. There's loads of water in ice at the poles.

- Deimos and Phobos were probably asteroids that were pulled in by the gravity of Mars. Phobos, the slightly larger moon, rises in the west and sets in the east and goes across the sky in 4.25 Earth hours. Deimos is so titchy it looks like a bright star.

- Olympus Mons is one of the highest mountains in the Solar System. It's a volcano, 600 km wide and 22 km high. That's nearly three times higher than that puny Earth pimple known as Mount Everest.

We decided to climb Olympus Mons starting at the top! Well, *really*! (Talk about tourists taking life easy – anyone would think they're on holiday!) To get enough energy, the Snotties snacked up on slime ice cream first.

Just then Sloppy decided she wanted to visit Deimos. Deimos is so small its gravity is very weak. We were almost weightless there!

Suddenly, Slobslime suffered a gut gas problem! In the weak gravity this was enough to blast her into space.

But Roverbot rushed to her rescue…

Five facts about Mars moons

1 The gravity in Deimos is so weak you can take off into space just by riding a bike. And Slobslime's super-strong bottom burp is sure to result in a blown-off blast-off.

2 If you want to see what Deimos looks like from Mars, try this exciting experiment. Ask a friend to hold a potato at one end of a football pitch. Seen from the other end of the football pitch, the potato looks the same size as Deimos as seen from Mars. Not very big, in other words. (If you're feeling cruel, you can wander off and leave your friend holding a potato for hours.)

3 Actually, Deimos even *looks* like a potato, although it won't make tasty French fries.

4 Each time Phobos orbits Mars, it spirals lower — dropping one metre every 100 Earth years. In 50 million years, the moon is due to hit Mars with messy results for any humans or aliens living there at the time.

5 In the 1950s, Ukrainian scientist Iosif Shmuelovich Shklovskii said that the moons of Mars were made by super-smart Martians. But in 1971, US space-probe photos proved that Phobos was just a large rock and the red-faced scientist said that he'd been joking.

ALIEN INVADERS

So what about those alien invaders and Mars monsters? Well, at present, we aren't sure that there are aliens in the Solar System at all. But some past astronomers have been mad-keen on the idea of Mars aliens. And some of them thought there may be life on Venus too. But, as I'm sure you've guessed, these claims were a bit too barmy to be believable...

CHEEKY CLAIMS
by Barmy Boffins

TEDIOUS TRUTH
by Luke Upwards

1 Swedish scientist Svante Arrhenius (1859–1927) said Venus was covered in swamps. Some scientists reckoned dinosaurs could live there.

2 In the 1830s, German astronomer, Franz von Paula Gruithuisen said Venus appears brighter every 47 years because the aliens light lamps in honour of their new emperor.

1 There's no water on Venus and it's hot enough to turn dinosaurs into instant tasty dino-dinners.

2 You'll know why Venus shines from page 67. Scientists aren't too sure why the brightness changes (if it does). But it's nothing to do with alien emperors.

But those spaced-out scientific suggestions sound normal compared with the most crazy, cheesy alien claim ever!

THE NEW YORK SUN
27 August 1835

GIANT BEAVER BOUNDS ABOUT ON MOON!

Sir J.H.

OUR ARTIST'S
IMPRESSION OF
THE BEAVER

Top astronomer Sir John Herschel has spotted a giant beaver on the Moon! "It walked on two feet and it didn't have a tail," gasped the awe-struck astronomer. Sir John said that the Moon is covered in trees and he's seen herds of hairy bison that waggle their ears, and ape-like humans with wings. "There's something unearthly about the whole scene — oh yes, silly me, that's because it's not Earth!" added Sir John.

A MESSAGE FROM THE EDITOR

Gee-whizz, we'd sure like to thank all you folks who've been buying our paper. We were on the edge of going bust, but since we started reporting these Moon discoveries, we've become the biggest-selling paper on the planet — yee ha!

116

And the truth? The staggering stories had been cooked up by reporter Richard Adams Locke (1800–1871). The real Sir John Herschel was in South Africa. When he got to hear of the *New York Sun*'s tall tales, he was confused, but then he started to laugh very loudly.

BUT WHAT ABOUT THE MARS MONSTERS?

Oh yes, thanks for reminding me! The most famous astronomer to believe in aliens on Mars was Percival Lowell (1855–1916). Now, as you can see from these dates, Percy's been pushing up the pansies for quite a few years. But I'm pleased to say that he's agreed to appear on the only TV show where the broadcast is live, even if the guests are dead...

Welcome to the TV show where we interview dead scientists.

GROAN!

DEAD BRAINY

R.I.P. PERCIVAL LOWELL 1855-1916

LIVE BROADCAST

Tonight, fresh from the grave, here's US astronomer Percival Lowell!

HOWDY!

Since you've been dead, quite a lot has happened...

SUCH AS?

That planet you said existed beyond Neptune...

YES! I SPENT YEARS LOOKING FOR IT, BUT I COULDN'T FIND IT!

It was found in 1930 – we call it Pluto and it's actually a dwarf planet! And you know those canals you saw on Mars?

YES, THEY WERE DUG BY BRAINY ALIENS TO BRING WATER TO THE DESERTS ON MARS.

The rotten reality is that when the two US Viking spacecraft landed on Mars in 1975 and 1976, they found that Mars is missing the basics for life. The sort of things you have at home – warmth, air and running water – don't exist on Mars. Trust Honest Bob to tell you the bad news – and then try to sell you the planet anyway…

HONEST BOB'S USED PLANETS

"Honest Bob was a lovely kid – as long as he was asleep he did nothing wrong." – Bob's mum.

MARS

REALLY COOL!

IDEAL SIZE!

NO DAMP!

LOVELY COLOUR!

- OK, so it's got 4.6 billion years on the clock. But that's what you might call a genuine antique – and it's real old too!
- It's not too big! I mean, it's cosy – some folk don't like a big planet.
- Real smart red colour to it. I deny that it's rust. OK – so the rocks are a bit rusty – but hey, that's all part of its character.
- It's a bit cold, but as my mum always says, a bit of cold won't kill you. Well, it will, but it's kinda healthy too!
- OK, so the planet's kinda dry at present, but at least you won't get rising-damp problems.

Why not take a trip to Mars and look at it for yourself? You'll love it!

LOW COST!

At only £700,000,000.12 – I'm robbing myself (instead of robbing you – OOPS pretend I didn't say that!).

THE TRUTH ABOUT HONEST BOB'S CLAIMS...

Don't be fooled by all that claptrap about 'cosy' Mars. The terrible truth is that Mars is too small for its own good. Billions of years ago, Mars had lots of air and water. The cosy air blanket kept Mars warm enough for running water. But, because Mars is smaller than Earth, the planet's gravity wasn't strong enough to hang on to the air. Ultraviolet rays from the Sun split the water into gases that wafted off into space. And that's why a visit to Mars is presently as pleasant as a pyjama party in a deep freeze.

What's that, Luke?

121

Luke Upwards writes…

> But give Bob his due – he's right about the rust. Iron in the rocks has rusted and that's why people call Mars 'the red planet'. If you get to see Mars from Earth, you'll find it even looks red from here!

So Mars isn't too nice right now – but is there any chance of life?

Surprisingly the answer isn't "No!" It's, "Hmm…" Well, that's what I think. But maybe you should judge for yourself? Yes, all you need to do is put on a judge's robe (a dressing gown will do fine). Take a chair in your very own courtroom (or even your bedroom) and listen to the arguments from our two top scientist-lawyers…

Putting the case for LIFE ON MARS is Izzie Starrs.

And putting the case against LIFE ON MARS is Luke Upwards.

Over to you, Luke!

Luke: Life on Mars? No way! I mean, the water's frozen solid – it's too cold. When the Viking spacecraft did robot tests on the soil, they couldn't prove that there was life.

Izzie: Objection, your honour! The tests showed chemical changes that might have been caused by microbes.

Luke: It was just a chemical reaction!

Time out to think it over: WHAT DO YOU THINK?

OK – now it's time for the case for life on Mars…

Izzie: So Mars is pretty dry now – but it once had lakes and rivers and where there's water, there's life. Maybe alien microbes hide in the ice or shelter in rocks underground.

Earth microbes can do this – so why not Martian microbes?

Luke: Objection, your honour. She said "maybe" – that means she's not sure!

MICROBES

Time out: WHAT DO YOU THINK?

Izzie: In 1996, some scientists found fossil microbes in a rock from Mars. Here's exhibit A.

Luke: Objection! That's just a grotty old lump of rock. These so-called fossil microbes are too small to have been real microbes.

Izzie: But they could be hairs that the microbes used to swim about. Chemical changes in the rock could have been caused by microbes!

Time out: WHAT DO YOU THINK?

Luke: OK – you asked for this! In 1932 a scientist said he'd found microbes in a rock from Mars. They were found to be microbes from human snot. Here's Exhibit B.

Izzie: That's gross!

TIME FOR OUR LAWYERS TO SUM UP...

Luke: There's no way that there's life on Mars. Even if there were once life (and there's no proof), it doesn't mean there's life now!

Izzie: It's possible that rocks with microbes in them could have been blasted from Mars and landed on Earth and brought life to Earth. We might have started off as aliens from Mars!

Luke: Are you calling me an alien from Mars?

Izzie: Well, you're slimy enough!

Hey, break it up, guys! It's only science and there's nothing at stake except our whole understanding of life and the way we see our place in the universe. Er – OK, that sounds rather a lot. OOOH DEAR! I bet that hurt, Luke!

BET YOU NEVER KNEW!

In 1995 Geneva University scientists Michel Mayor and Didier Queloz spotted a wobble in star 51-Pegasi caused by a planet's gravity. That planet is now called Dimidium. Scientists have spotted thousands more exoplanets (as they are known). Most are HORRIBLE – Dimidium is red-hot, some exoplanets have gravity strong enough to break your bones and some are covered in scalding steam. In 2013 scientists even spotted an exoplanet being eaten by a black hole. But other exoplanets appear like Earth – so they could have alien life lurking on them...

TIME TO ROCK ON

These arguments look set to run – so let's make a run ourselves … to the asteroid belt. Asteroids are rubbly leftovers from when the Solar System formed…

HUH?

WELCOME TO THE
ASTEROID BELT
PLEASE DRIVE CAREFULLY

But not that close together! There are over one million asteroids but they're separated by millions of kilometres of space. And here's a few more facts to get you rocking…

Space, stars and slimy aliens fact file

Name: Asteroids

The basic facts:

1 Most asteroids are shaped like, er, rocks.

2 The asteroid belt contains the dwarf planet Ceres. Found by Italian Guiseppe Piazzi in 1801, Ceres is 950 km across. There's hardly any atmosphere but there are rocks, ice and maybe an ocean under the ice. Some scientists think it might be home to alien life.

3 There are enough asteroids out there to make a planet the size of the Moon, or even bigger.

4 Unfortunately, Jupiter's gravity knocked the asteroids together and smashed them to bits so they didn't get the chance to make a planet. Poor little darlings!

5 In 2000, scientists found an asteroid shaped like a dog's bone.

6 Some asteroids are in two lumps loosely stuck together by gravity. Others even have their own mini moons the size of footballs.

Slimy secret:

Do YOU wanna be rich? Many asteroids contain valuable minerals such as iron and platinum. They're worth billions. Send a spacecraft to fetch one and you'll be the richest person in the Solar System. (Honest Bob's working on it right now!)

THE NAME GAME QUIZ

With so many asteroids zooming around up there, is it any wonder that astronomers are running out of names for them! Which two items from this list haven't had asteroids named after them?

1 Mr Spock, the character from the TV series *Star Trek*.

2 A type of pudding.

ASTEROID AND CUSTARD

YUMMY!

HUH?

3 A shipping company.

4 A pop group.

5 A well-known brand of washing powder.

| ANSWERS |

Made up

1 There IS an asteroid called Mr Spock but it was named after an astronomer's ginger cat! The cat was named after the TV character – so you can have half a point if you said TRUE.

5 I guess this idea didn't wash with astronomers.

True

2 Halawe is a sweet eaten in the Middle East. It's a tasty blend of sugar, ground sesame seeds and lemon juice. But if you sink your teeth into Halawe the asteroid by mistake, your teeth will fall out!

3 Hapag was a German shipping company.

4 Yes, it's the only place in the universe that you can still see the famous 1960s pop group The Beatles together. So let's have a big cheer for asteroids Lennon, McCartney, Harrison and Starr. Shame they can't sing.

Phew – at last we're safely through the asteroid belt. Now for the big one. It's time to hit Jupiter! Well, let's hope we don't actually *hit* the planet. That might be a teeny-weeny bit fatal…

GIANT JUPITER AND SHOW-OFF SATURN

If Jupiter were human, he'd be a big bullying crook and the moons would be his gang. So, let's meet the roughest, toughest gangster gang in the Solar System.

THE JUPITER GANG

BIG J →

IO →

EUROPA

CALLISTO

GANYMEDE

Yes, Big J's a planet-sized bully. He's so awful, the cosmic cops are after him…

THE MEMOIRS OF DETECTIVE PLANET OF THE SSPD

Yeah, I remember Big J. He was a nasty big-time crime boss over on the wrong side of the Solar System. You couldn't miss him - he had this big red spot on his face and I figure he'd been eating too many asteroids because his waist sure was bulging.

Now, Big J was a big, mean fella - I mean he had real gravity. He had a gang of four big moons. There are also loads of smaller moons, but they were small fry - little more than hangers-on. Anyhow, we got complaints that Big J was turning the heat on one of his own gang members, a moon called Io. Poor Io was melting inside thanks to Big J's gravity, helped out by the rest of the gang. What a crowd of sickos! Then the finger was pointed at Big J for picking up asteroids by gravity and firing them in the general direction of Earth. Yessir - Jupiter was the meanest critter I ever met in my years of cosmic crime-fighting. He was always armed and dangerous. He had a radiation gun. Hey - don't ask me how it works, I'm just a cop. Big J picked up radiation from the Sun using some kind of magnetic force. And this low-life scumbag planet blasted all the moons around him! He even blasted his next-door neighbour, Mr Saturn! The best thing to do with Big J was to lock him away and throw away the key!

GET THE MESSAGE?

Jupiter is more antisocial than a slug in a salad bar.

And now it's time for another incredible instalment of our sci-fi space story. In their tour of the Solar System, the aliens have reached Jupiter…

Oddblob's Alien Adventure

Jupiter is dangerous. The very idea of going there gave both my brainy brains a hammering headache. But, for some stupid reason, those half-witted Snotty space tourists wanted to take a closer look. Too close for safety!

BLURBI—DATA

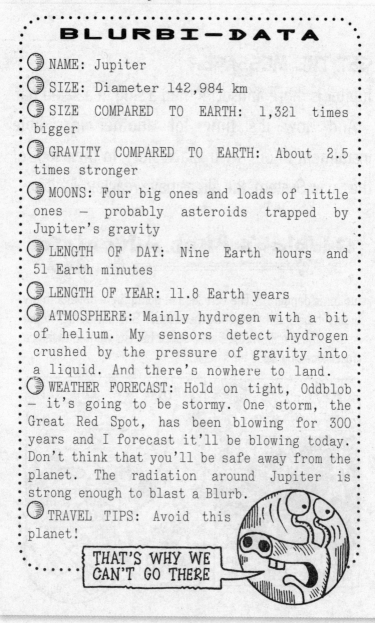

NAME: Jupiter

SIZE: Diameter 142,984 km

SIZE COMPARED TO EARTH: 1,321 times bigger

GRAVITY COMPARED TO EARTH: About 2.5 times stronger

MOONS: Four big ones and loads of little ones — probably asteroids trapped by Jupiter's gravity

LENGTH OF DAY: Nine Earth hours and 51 Earth minutes

LENGTH OF YEAR: 11.8 Earth years

ATMOSPHERE: Mainly hydrogen with a bit of helium. My sensors detect hydrogen crushed by the pressure of gravity into a liquid. And there's nowhere to land.

WEATHER FORECAST: Hold on tight, Oddblob — it's going to be stormy. One storm, the Great Red Spot, has been blowing for 300 years and I forecast it'll be blowing today. Don't think that you'll be safe away from the planet. The radiation around Jupiter is strong enough to blast a Blurb.

TRAVEL TIPS: Avoid this planet!

THAT'S WHY WE CAN'T GO THERE

And with that I pointed out the things we could see from a safe distance.

- Bulging middle – Jupiter spins so fast that it bulges a bit in the middle.

- Dark bands of clouds caused by areas of cooler gas that sink towards the planet.

- Great Red Spot – The winds in this stormy area are strong enough to flatten a skyscraper. Sometimes the spot turns grey – maybe Jupiter uses anti-spot cream, snirk, snirk.

Hmm – bulging middle, big red spot. Jupiter reminded me of Slobslime, except she had a big green spot. By now, the Snotties had lost interest in Jupiter and were eyeing up Europa with all three of their eyes.

We decided to land on Europa for a spot of space skating. Snotties are fond of this sport because they can glide along without much effort...

At this very moment, an asteroid crashed into Europa and made a hole in the ice. And, of course, Slobslime fell in! The ice is many kilometres thick, but beneath it

there is an ocean up to 100 km deep. After Slobslime fell in, the ice quickly froze above her in the cold of space. There was only one thing we could do … and that was nothing!

In the end I had to rescue Slobslime to shut Sloppy up. So I fired the spacecraft's engine to melt the ice and grabbed Slobslime from the water.

The icy cold instantly froze Slobslime into a block of ice. And while she was melting I decided we'd all had enough of Europa.

IMPORTANT SCIENTIFIC NOTE
Like the ocean on Ceres, Europa's ocean might be home to life. There could be alien microbes or giant worms (similar to creatures that lurk in Earth's deep oceans). But Oddblob didn't even look for them... What a shame!

AMAZING MOONS

Even without the worms, Jupiter's moons are awfully odd. So here's a really odd thought to amuse you. What would Jupiter moons *taste* like? Welcome to the Solar System's first cosmic cook book!

The Cosmic Cook Book

Hi to all you intergalactic gourmets! If you're feeling hungry, why not treat yourself to these tasty recipes ... they're cooked just the way old Jupiter likes 'em!

Io pizza

Ingredients:
Several million tonnes of rock
Sulphur (according to taste)
Hydrogen

1 Mix the ingredients and place close to (about 421,600 km away from) a pre-heated Jupiter with its gravity and radiation going full blast.

2 Leave for 4.6 billion years, while Jupiter cooks the mixture until the rocks melt.

WARNING ~ The mixture will get very hot (up to 500°C in places) and its insides will bubble up to the surface. They'll stink of rotting eggs but it's all part of the flavour!

Europa slushy-melt

Ingredients:
Several million tonnes of rock
Enough water to fill all of Earth's oceans
Alien microbe slime and giant worms
(if you like that sort of thing)

URGH!

1 Form the rock into a ball and pour on the water.
2 Freeze until the outside is frozen solid but the inside is still runny.
Alternatives
For a more crunchy mixture, try the Callisto method. You freeze the ice a little more and crack it a bit. Or you can simply mix the rock and ice into a ball (the Ganymede method).
It really is that simple.
Enjoy your moons and *bon appetit!*

Oh, so you didn't fancy munching one of Jupiter's moons? I guess it's time to make our escape from Jupiter and shoot off to Saturn. And by some curious coincidence, the next episode of our space story is set there...

Oddblob's Alien Adventure

Slobslime thawed out of her ice block in time to see Saturn. Of course, the brainless alien was confused by the rings.

WOW — THAT'S AN EARTHLING IN A HAT!

With a big sigh, I asked Cosmo for the low-down on Saturn. With an equally big sigh, Cosmo replied...

BLURBI-DATA

🪐 NAME: Saturn

🪐 SIZE: Diameter 116,464 km

🪐 SIZE COMPARED TO EARTH: 764 times bigger

🪐 GRAVITY COMPARED TO EARTH: Only 1.16 times as much. That's because Saturn is mostly made up of light gas with weak gravity. The whole planet is light enough to float on water!

🪐 MOONS: I had a dreadful job trying to count them. There are more than sixty but only thirteen have a diameter larger than 50 km. The largest moon, Titan, is 5,150 km in diameter.

🪐 LENGTH OF DAY: 10 Earth hours and 38 Earth minutes

🪐 LENGTH OF YEAR: 29.5 Earth years

🪐 ATMOSPHERE: Hydrogen and helium, like Jupiter

🪐 WEATHER FORECAST: EXTREME WEATHER WARNING! The winds reach 1,800 km an hour. There's no solid surface to land on and there's a danger of being seasick or airsick or both. Probably at the same time.

🪐 TRAVEL TIPS: Take a giant windbreak and a large supply of sick bags.

We got a great view of Saturn's rings and I told the Snotties there are thousands of rings and how each one is made of shiny bits of ice and rock. They may have come from a crashed comet. Moons move between the rings and their gravity holds the rings together...

Then I realized that the Snotties weren't listening.

BITS OF ROCK AND ICE VARY IN SIZE!

GRRR!

SNORE!

ZZZZ

I decided to wake up those snoring Snotties…

We Blurbs love Blurbi-kite-flying. Unfortunately, the winds of Saturn proved just a bit too strong…

Lucky old Oddblob! Don't you wish you could see Saturn's rings close up? Of course, you can see the real thing if you happen to be looking through a really good telescope. But if you don't have a really good telescope, here's the next best thing:

DARE YOU DISCOVER ... SATURN'S RINGS?
You will need:

A BALL — 7 CM ACROSS

AN UNDERSTANDING FRIEND →

CARD

← SCISSORS

STICKY TAPE

RULER →

PENCIL →

COMPASS FOR DRAWING CIRCLES OR AN 18-CM CIRCLE THAT YOU CAN DRAW ROUND (PLATES AND SAUCERS ARE GOOD FOR THIS)

What you do:

1 Using the compass, or an object to draw round, draw a circle on the card 18 cm across. The circle should be 11 cm wider than the ball. Cut the circle out.

2 Cut out the inside of the card circle to make a card ring.

18 cm   10 cm

PLATE NOW HAS
LARGE PIECE OF
CHOCCY CAKE ON IT!

3 Stick your card ring to the ball with sticky tape.

4 Well done, you've just made Saturn! Ask your friend to hold it in their hand and stand 15 metres away from you. They should start by holding the planet level and then at an angle.

You should notice:

When the rings are held level you can't see them. They're too thin and far away. The real Saturn's the same. Saturn spins at an angle, and every 15 years the rings cannot be seen from Earth. In fact, we're looking at Saturn sideways on.

But they appear when seen from any other angle…

BET YOU NEVER KNEW!

Saturn's rings are 270,000 km wide, but only 30 metres thick. If you put the rings in a giant shrinking machine and shrank them to the size of a cricket or baseball pitch, they'd be no thicker than this page.

THAT MOON'S THE LIMIT

But let's drag our eyeballs away from the rings. I've got some BIG news! Honest Bob's just sold me a ticket to the biggest night out in the Solar System.

It's Saturn's Odd Moons Awards. It's like the Hollywood Oscars in space!

SATURN'S ODD MOONS AWARDS

All the stars are out in force for this glittering galactic event! And the awards for the oddest moon prizes for Saturn are as follows...

THE CRAZIEST MOON couple award goes to ... Janus and Epimetheus. Hey, what's up with these guys? Every four years they swap orbits. Are they getting bored or something?

CRAZIEST MOON

UGLIEST MOON

THE UGLIEST MOON award goes to ... Tethys. This moon has a crack running halfway around it. Anyone know a planet plastic surgeon?

THE MOST TASTY-LOOKING MOON award goes to ... Hyperion. It's shaped like a giant hamburger. Fast food anyone?

THE BEST-DRESSED MOON award goes to ... Iapetus. This moon is wearing a lovely stripy black-and-white zebra-style outfit. Very trendy – give us a twirl!

And now for the one we've all been waiting for! The award for THE MADDEST MOON ON SATURN...

And the winner is ... TITAN with its hazy orange nitrogen atmosphere, ice mountains, methane seas and volcanoes blasting water and ammonia (a substance found in rotten wee). It even rains methane. No other moon has anything like this. You can find methane in cow farts but Titan must be the ultimate loony moo-moon!

I'D LIKE TO THANK EVERYONE WHO'S HELPED ME IN THE LAST FOUR BILLION YEARS, ESPECIALLY SATURN. JUST BECAUSE I'M –180°C SOME PEOPLE THINK I'M A BIT COLD. BUT I'M REAL FRIENDLY AND OFFER A WARM WELCOME, JUST SO LONG AS YOU DON'T MIND FREEZING TO DEATH.

And I do hope you don't mind a bit of freezing. You see, the remaining planets on our tour of the Solar System are chilly and cold with a c-c-capital C! D-dare you take a look?

YOU CAN BORROW ONE OF MY BLURBI BOBBLE-HATS!

ODDBALL OUTER PLANETS

The wonderful thing about the Solar System is that you can be really weird and wacky and way out and no one seems to mind. And they don't come weirder, wackier or further-out that those kooky, chilly planets – Uranus, Neptune and the puny dwarf planets beyond…

Take Uranus, for example. This planet is seriously way out. It's way out from the Sun by about 2,871 million km. And it's so weird and way out that instead of spinning, it tumbles head over heels through space like an out-of-control acrobat. I bet even Honest Bob would find Uranus a hard planet to sell…

HONEST BOB'S USED PLANETS

"My Bob never tells a single lie - he normally tells lots of them." – Bob's mum.

URANUS

What a cute mover – that planet's got style! No, sir, they don't make 'em like this any more! You'll be the envy of all your buddies when you take this planet, with its unique head-over-heels motion, for a roll!

ENJOY LONG, HOT SUMMERS!

If you're sitting at its south pole, you get 42 Earth years of summer when the Sun never sets – followed by 42 years of winter. Oh, dang! I wasn't going to mention the winter! Anyway, it's yours for £11,000,000,000.12 and it's a steal – even if I say so myself!

Hmm, Uranus sounds kinda fun! Let's get back to our sci-fi space story as the aliens whizz towards the planet… What will Oddblob make of oddball Uranus?

Oddblob's Alien Adventure

We were nearing the end of our tour of the Solar System and I wasn't going to be sad to see the Snotties go. I wondered how I'd ever clean that sticky green slime out of my spacecraft!

The next planet we were going to visit was Uranus, but it was just going to be a fly-by. Cosmo had the details – and landing was a bad idea...

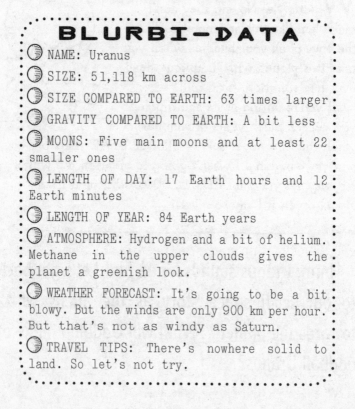

BLURBI-DATA

- NAME: Uranus
- SIZE: 51,118 km across
- SIZE COMPARED TO EARTH: 63 times larger
- GRAVITY COMPARED TO EARTH: A bit less
- MOONS: Five main moons and at least 22 smaller ones
- LENGTH OF DAY: 17 Earth hours and 12 Earth minutes
- LENGTH OF YEAR: 84 Earth years
- ATMOSPHERE: Hydrogen and a bit of helium. Methane in the upper clouds gives the planet a greenish look.
- WEATHER FORECAST: It's going to be a bit blowy. But the winds are only 900 km per hour. But that's not as windy as Saturn.
- TRAVEL TIPS: There's nowhere solid to land. So let's not try.

To be honest, I didn't like Uranus. Its colour reminded me of a spacesick Snotty. The moons looked as boring as an unwanted Blurbi-mas present. I showed the Snotties the best bits – and it didn't take long…

• Uranus has rings like Saturn. But they're only 1.6 km thick and made of black rocks, so they're hard to spot.

• One of the moons – Miranda – has grooves that look like racetracks. That's groovy – snirk, snirk. One of these is called the chevron! Miranda was probably smashed apart by an asteroid and pulled itself back together by gravity.

BET YOU NEVER KNEW!

1 Some of the moons of Uranus are named after characters in plays by William Shakespeare. For example, Titania and Oberon are from *A Midsummer's Night Dream*. There's also a character in the play called Bottom, but scientists seem to have 'backed out' of naming a moon after him!

2 Another moon goes by the name of Puck. On Puck you'll find craters called Lob, Butz and Bogle. And no, I didn't make up those names!

HOW TO FIND A PLANET IN ABOUT 23 EASY STAGES

Now, here's a quick question to bamboozle your brain. How many astronomers does it take to discover a planet?

Well, in the case of Neptune, the answer is "quite a few"… But that's not too surprising because, from Earth, Neptune looks like just another star. It's as hard to spot as a needle in a … pin factory.

After a long search, Neptune was eventually tracked down by young scientists, John Couch Adams (1819–1892) and Urbain Le Verrier (1811–1877). We've put them in two rooms, so they can tell their stories separately. These stories begin in 1841, when no one knew that Neptune

ADAMS' STORY

LE VERRIER'S STORY

YEAR 1841

ADAMS' STORY: I reckon there's a planet beyond Uranus. Uranus is being pulled forward and then slowed down by this planet's gravity. This makes Uranus change speed.

LE VERRIER'S STORY: I haven't really thought about anything so far – certainly not a new planet.

1845

ADAMS' STORY: I've worked out where the new planet is! I'll ask astronomer, George Airy, to find it for me.

LE VERRIER'S STORY: I reckon there's a planet beyond Uranus and I know where it is. I've written about it in a scientific journal. I'll ask top astronomers in Paris to find it for me.

1846	*Grr — he's not looking! I've called round to see Airy three times but he's never at home.*	Grrr - they're not looking for the planet either so I'm sending my ideas to some astronomer pals in Berlin, Germany.
LATER IN 1846	*Airy's read my ideas at last and he's asked ace astronomer James Challis to look for the new planet. But so far, nothing. I'm going to miss out on the glory!*	Hurrah! The Germans have found the new planet. It's just where I said it was. I'M GOING TO GET THE GLORY!!! CHEERS!

So who actually discovered Neptune? Was it…?

a) Adams. He was the first person to suggest where the planet was.

b) Le Verrier. He made sure the planet was spotted. And in science the credit for a discovery goes to the first person to write about it in a scientific journal – which was Le Verrier.

or **c)** German astronomers Johann Galle and Heinrich d'Arrest. They were the first to find Neptune. Well, Luke?

Most astronomers would say Adams and Le Verrier. But some people would say the answer's d) Galileo! The incredible Italian spotted Neptune through his telescope long before anyone else, but he thought it was a star rather than a planet.

Anyway, you'll be pleased to know that when Adams and Le Verrier actually met they became friends, despite not speaking each other's language. (Hmm – Le Verrier was said to have been the rudest man in France, so it may have helped that Adams didn't know what he was saying…)

*WE'VE TRANSLATED HIS FRENCH INTO ENGLISH

Now, you might think that discovering Neptune sounded a tricky business. But the details of the discovery were even more mixed-up than I've made out so far. It's almost as if Neptune *didn't want to be found!*

YEAH — LEAVE ME ALONE!

Before Adams, lots of people thought there was a planet beyond Uranus, but none of them found time to look for it.

COULDN'T BE BOTHERED, MORE LIKE!

James Challis did see Neptune but he thought it was a star. On the evening that he would have got his best view of the planet, he was drinking tea with a friend.

HA, HA! YOU MISSED YOUR CHANCE, MATE!

The boss of the Berlin Observatory, Johann Encke (1791–1865), also missed out on seeing the planet because he was at a party.

'SPACED OUT' ON CHAMPAGNE, I EXPECT!

And now back to our space story. Will the aliens have trouble finding Neptune?

Oddblob's Alien Adventure

With the aid of Cosmo's hyper-speed multi-dimensional navigation systems, I had no difficulties in finding Neptune. The planet looked like Uranus. In fact, it looked enough like Uranus to fool the Snotties…

BEEN THERE! DUNNIT!

I pointed out that Neptune's methane clouds are easier to see. Pah! – any alien can spot the difference! I asked Cosmo for the facts. And I made sure the Snotties paid attention.

BLURBI-DATA

- NAME: Neptune
- SIZE: Diameter 49,244 km
- SIZE COMPARED TO EARTH: 58 times larger
- GRAVITY COMPARED TO EARTH: A bit stronger than Earth – and Uranus
- MOONS: I counted 14 moons. Triton (diameter 2,710 km) is the only large one.
- LENGTH OF DAY: 16 Earth hours and 6 Earth minutes
- LENGTH OF YEAR: 165 Earth years
- ATMOSPHERE: Mostly hydrogen, some helium and a smidgen of methane

🌑 WEATHER FORECAST: EXTRA EXTREME WEATHER WARNING! It's going to be more stormy than Saturn! Expect winds of 2,000 km an hour – so put that kite away, Oddblob! There'll be methane-snow high in the atmosphere, but it'll melt before it lands.

🌑 TRAVEL TIPS: If you dare go near Neptune, Oddblob, I'll erase all your computer games!

Once more we hovered at a safe distance while I pointed out the tourist attractions…

- Neptune has four rings (they're dark and hard to see).
- There's a storm the size of Earth called the Great Dark Spot that travels round the planet backwards.
- There's a cloud called the Scooter that blows around the planet faster than the Spot.

- Hot spots at the poles produce gas. The gas turns into a rain of diamonds. I told the snotties that catching diamonds was too dangerous.

- Triton is the only moon in the Solar System that orbits in the opposite direction to its planet's spin. The pink south pole is made of frozen nitrogen and the rest of the moon is covered in ice.

When the Snotties heard about Triton's ice, they wanted to go there. They enjoyed skating on Europa so much that they wanted to skate on Triton. But Cosmo warned us that Triton is −235°C. It's the coldest place in the Solar System and it could be too cold to visit safely. But did the Snotties listen?

As it happened, the Snotties had great fun skating on the frozen moon. And, for once, there were no problems… Until it was time to leave…

THE ENGINE'S FROZEN! I CAN'T GET IT STARTED!

PRESS! PRESS!

A few hours later…

M-M-MY S-S-SLIME IS F-F-FROZEN!

SHIVER!

BRRRRR!

But just then…

As luck would have it, the spacecraft was parked on a nitrogen geyser. This is a hole where liquid nitrogen blasts from the ground. It's like a hot-water geyser on Earth. The blasting nitrogen turned to gas – it was enough to throw us into space and get our engines going.

And so we set off to the dwarf planet Pluto…

The first thing to say about Pluto is that it's *really* far away – on average, 5,193 MILLION km. No wonder the US astronomer who found it, Clyde Tombaugh (1906–1997), had to check 45 million stars over 13 years to see which one moved like a planet. I bet he got a stiff neck.

SPOT THE DISCOVERER OF PLUTO

AN INTERESTING IDEA FOR YOUNGER READERS

Mind you, there's one thing harder than finding a new dwarf planet – and that's thinking up a name for it! Imagine you had to think up names for places near you. Perhaps you'd name them after your friends…

You could name a putrid-smelling pond after your brother or sister. And you could name a dismal dump after your teacher (or is that a rubbish idea?).

But someone's sure to challenge your choice of names…

GRRR — NAME A DUMP AFTER ME, WOULD YOU?

Things were much the same with the dwarf planet Clyde Tombaugh found...

At that time everyone thought it was a full-sized planet and everyone had an idea what to call it. Remember Percival Lowell from page 117? Well, his wife wanted the new discovery to be named Lowell after him (it's better than Planet Percy). Then she decided it ought be called Constance after herself.

Astronomers hated Constance's idea. The other planets had been named after ancient Roman gods like Mars and Jupiter.

169

Things were just turning nasty when someone in England came up with a better name. Incredibly that someone was just 11 years old. She was a girl named Venetia Burney.

How I named a new planet by Venetia Burney

We've been doing planets in school. One day, my teacher, Mr Smith, stuck a yellow circle on the playground wall. It was as wide as my arm long.

"That's the Sun," he explained. "And now

we're going for a walk to find out how far away the planets are."

Mr Smith led us across the playground. He was counting out the paces. He walked so fast, his shoes started squeaking. When he reached 30, he bent down and laid a teeny little seed on the ground.

"That's Marcury," he announced, puffing a bit. "Cor - isn't it little?" we said, squinting at the tiny seed.

And that's how I learned that the planets are really small compared to the Sun. And they're a long way apart. The Earth turned out to be a squishy pea on the pavement outside the school. We looked back at the Sun and it looked quite small now. Then my friend Amy trod on the pea by mistake.

"You've just squashed the world!" I said. "Aarggh - a giant foot's just landed on top of us and splatted us flat!"

We headed all the way down the street and across the park until we reached Saturn. There seemed no end to the Solar System. Mr Smith was puffing like a train and his shoes sounded like a couple of noisy mice having a fight. His face was the colour of a sweaty tomato and he was mopping his forehead with a big spotted handkerchief.

"1,019 paces!" gasped Mr Smith. "And this golf ball's Saturn."

We couldn't even see our Sun circle but Mr Smith said that, from the real Saturn, the Sun would just look like a bright star.

"I bet it's cold on Saturn," said Amy with a shiver.

Our teacher was examining his watch. "We'll have to leave it there - Uranus is twice as far from the Sun as Saturn. And Neptune is three times further."

I was glad Mr Smith didn't make walk to Neptune.

PHEW!

In the afternoon, Mr Smith taught us about the ancient Roman gods. And that's how I knew that the planets were named after gods, but I noticed that some gods didn't have their own planets.

where's my planet?

JUPITER   VENUS   MERCURY   PLUTO

I first heard about the new planet a few weeks later. Mum, Dad, Grandpa and me were having breakfast. As usual, Grandpa was reading the newspaper aloud and, as usual, the news was boring. I was munching my toast loudly so that I wouldn't have to listen. Dad gave me an annoyed look.

"Don't eat so loudly, Venetia," he said.

But just then, Grandpa read something about a new planet and my ears pricked up.

"It's a wonderful discovery," Grandpa was saying. "But astronomers don't know what to call it. The new planet is a very long way from the Sun..."

And that's when I had my great idea.

"I think Pluto would be a good name for it!" I said.

"Don't speak with your mouth full!" said Mum sharply.

I knew Pluto was the Roman god of the underworld and I thought the underworld must be cold and dark like the planet.

But Grandpa was looking at me with interest.

"Well, bless me!" he exclaimed, laying his newspaper on the table. "What a good name for the planet! I must make a note of it. I'll call on my old friend

Mr Turner at the University Observatory and see what he thinks of it."

Mr Turner liked the name so much he sent a special telegram to Mr Tombaugh, the astronomer who found the planet. And all Mr Tombaugh's astronomer friends liked the name so much they decided to use it.

Thinking up planet names is easy! I can't wait for the next planet to be discovered. But there's NO WAY I want to walk there!

Mr Tombaugh

BET YOU NEVER KNEW!

If Venetia's teacher had made the children walk to Pluto, they'd have found a pinhead over 3.7 km from the school. No wonder the real Pluto was so hard to track down! But it was harder because Pluto's orbit is so awesomely odd. It's a stretched-out ellipse that takes Pluto up to 7,390 million km from the Sun.

YOU'RE FAR OUT, MAN!

YEAH, IT'S COSMIC, DUDE!

SUN

NEPTUNE'S ORBIT

PLUTO'S ORBIT

Despite the distance, Clyde Tombaugh got to visit Pluto – sort of. In 2006 a space probe set off for Pluto. It carried the astronomer's ashes. Meanwhile, back in our space story, the aliens are off to Pluto and the snotties aren't happy...

Oddblob's Alien Adventure

We spent half the day travelling to Pluto. And, after five minutes, the Snotties were showing signs of boredom.

When, at last, Pluto came in sight, the Snotties weren't impressed.

I asked Cosmo for details. The Snotties were right ... Pluto was pathetic!

They protested that Pluto looked too cold. And they hadn't warmed up after Triton!

BLURBI-DATA

◐ NAME: Pluto

◐ SIZE: Diameter 2,370 km

◐ SIZE COMPARED TO EARTH: You could fit 160 Plutos inside the Earth with room to spare

◐ GRAVITY COMPARED TO EARTH: Next to nothing

◐ MOONS: Five. The largest, Charon, takes one Pluto day to orbit the dwarf planet. If you're on Pluto, the moon is always in the same place in the sky.

◐ LENGTH OF DAY: Six Earth days and nine and a half Earth hours.

◐ LENGTH OF YEAR: 248 Earth years

◐ ATMOSPHERE: A bit of methane and nitrogen

◐ WEATHER FORECAST: There's hardly any sunshine so it's going to be FREEZING COLD — forever! There are nitrogen ice plains, watery ice mountains and frozen methane spikes hundreds of metres tall!

◐ TRAVEL TIPS: Take a spacesuit and plenty of hot drinks.

So Pluto *was* cold. But it was my type of planet – peace, quiet and awesome scenery. But as we whizzed over the icy red surface those snot-brained snotties wouldn't shut up about the cold.

Well, if Pluto's too chilly for you why not dance to keep warm? This science dance shows why Pluto and Charon are always facing each other...

DARE YOU DISCOVER ... THE PLUTO SPIN?

What you need:

• Two people, ideally an adult parent or teacher, and you! (The adult is going to be Pluto and you are going to be Charon.)

• Some groovy music

WARNING TO YOUNGER READERS
All you need to know is that Pluto's bigger than you.
Don't ask the adult how much they weigh!

What you do:

1 Pluto should put both their hands round Charon's hands and hold tight.

2 Put the music on...

3 Start swinging round and round...

Hold your partner by the hands
And start swinging round and round!
ROUND AND ROUND AND ROUND YOU GO
'Cos you're spinning like old Pluto!

You should notice:

Wheee! This is FUN! Charon's swinging around in a bigger circle than Pluto. Pluto's gravity is strong enough to swing Charon in a bigger circle and hold it in position.

The snotties have had enough but there's plenty more to see. In fact, Pluto is just one of thousands of frozen-rocky thingies in the Kuiper-Edgeworth belt including the dwarf planet Eris. And here's what they missed. Eris is roughly the same size as Pluto, has one moon and takes 557 years to orbit the Sun – so baby Sloppy would have to wait forever for her birthday slimy-cake.

There are many more dwarf planets and some are named after Pacific island gods. I bet you never knew that Haumea was originally called 'Santa' and Makemake was known as 'Easter Bunny'.

Another icy world, Quaoar (Kwar-o-ar), gets its name from a native American god. Quaoar was a god of the Tongva tribe who used to live in the Los Angeles area of the USA. That's funny – I thought it was the sound you make when a dentist tells you to "open wide".

Carry on travelling and you get to the Oort cloud. Jan Oort was a Dutch stargazer who suggested this vast area of icy rocks existed. (Estonian astronomer Ernst Öpik had the same idea but didn't get the glory.) Mind you, the rocks are far more spaced-out than in our crazy cartoon!

CRUEL COMETS

The Oort cloud stretches a quarter of the distance to our nearest star – Proxima Centauri. Those space snowballs sound fantastically far away but they can come closer to home. That's when we call them 'comets'. Here's what happens…

1 A distant star gives a comet a nudge with its gravity.

2 The nudge sends the comet whizzing in the direction of the Sun.

3 As the comet nears the Sun, it starts to melt and

the solar wind blows tails of gas millions of kilometres behind it. The solar wind ensures that the gas tail always points directly away from the Sun.

Every year, Earth whizzes through clouds of melted comet dust and rock. Then, we see free light shows called meteor showers as the dust and rock burns up in our atmosphere. The meteors make tiny whizzy flashes of light high in the night sky. And it's really exciting counting them and trying to guess where the next one will appear. Here are the best times to see them…

You can see the meteors anywhere in the sky, especially in the eastern half.

Of course, these bits of comet are too small to harm Earth. For that we'd need to be smashed by something really big. Something like an asteroid ... but there's not much danger of that! Er – hold on – let's check the sci-fi story. What's happening on Oddblob's spacecraft...?

Oddblob's Alien Adventure

BLURBI-MESSAGE

A HUGE ASTEROID IS HEADING FOR EARTH. THIS COULD BE THE END OF LIFE AS WE KNOW IT!

OH THAT SOUNDS INTERESTING...

OOPS – I spoke too soon! You'd better carry on reading ... otherwise you'll miss the end of the world!

THE END-OF-THE-WORLD MOVIE SHOW

There's nothing movie makers like more than a nice Earth-shattering disaster. Something with a budget of billions and big bangs and stunning special effects. But what's the true picture? Are we really going to be destroyed from space? And, oh yes, what's going to happen in our sci-fi space story?

Well, you'll be delighted to know that the answers to all these questions are in this chapter … so read on!

The first thing to say is that most movies about the Earth being wiped out from space are STUPID. The science is WRONG with a capital W – they just couldn't happen in real life.

SPOT THE SILLY SCIENCE SCREEN QUIZ

Here's a selection of movies from Honest Bob's Used DVD store.

1 Which five really could happen and which three sound like silly science and couldn't ever happen in a Pluto year of Sundays?

2 Which of these movies could come true some time in the next hundred years?

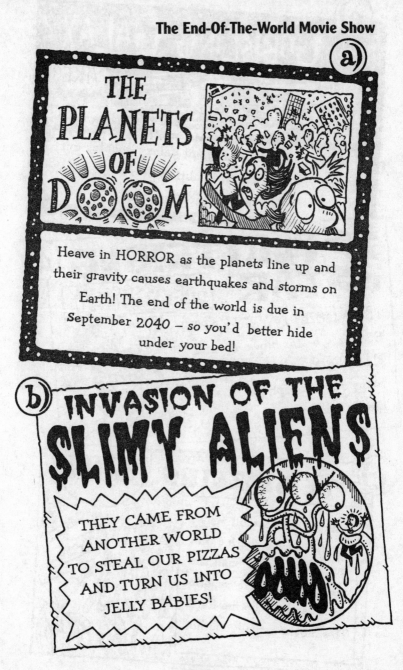

a)

THE PLANETS OF DOOM

Heave in HORROR as the planets line up and their gravity causes earthquakes and storms on Earth! The end of the world is due in September 2040 – so you'd better hide under your bed!

b)

INVASION OF THE SLIMY ALIENS

THEY CAME FROM ANOTHER WORLD TO STEAL OUR PIZZAS AND TURN US INTO JELLY BABIES!

c) THE GOBBLING GALAXY

ARGH!
HELP!
YIKES!
EEK!

Gasp in horror as a giant galaxy gobbles our Milky Way and Earth is hurled into a black hole! It's a hole lot of horror!

THE SPLATTERING STAR d)

WE'RE GONNA DIE LAUGHING!!!

IT'S A QUIET DAY ON EARTH... Suddenly, a star blows up and blasts Earth with radiation that turns our atmosphere into laughing gas!

e) THE SIZZLING SUN

Experience the ultimate suntan as you see the Sun turn into a red fireball and melt Mercury and vaporize Venus and eat up the Earth. This movie's really red-hot!

f) "THE" "SMASHING" "METEOR" "SHOWER"

Tremble in terror as millions of people get hit on the head by stunning space rocks!

g) THE CRUSHING COMET CRASH

Shudder and shriek as a huge comet crashes into Earth and blasts billions of people to bits.

ASTEROID ATTACK **h)**

Shout with shock as the Earth is smashed by a giant space rock and all life is wiped out!

OOER!

ANSWERS

1 Scientifically possible movies – **c)**, **d)**, **e)**, **g)** and **h)**. Impossible movies – **a)**, **b)**, **f)**.
2 The movie that might happen in real life in the next hundred years is **h)**.

Now, I bet you want to know why some of the movies are possible and why some of them are as likely as a vegetarian vampire bat… Well, with Luke's help, I've got the answers. Let's start with the movies that just couldn't happen.

Three ways the Earth WON'T get wiped out…
1 The planets lining up

In 2000, the planets appeared close together as seen from Earth. Some people were afraid their gravity would pull on the Earth and cause disaster. So, what happened? Not a lot. The effect on us was weaker than the gravity of the Sun and the Moon. The next time this is due to occur will be in 2040.

2 Alien invasion

As Luke was quick to remind me, there's no proof that aliens exist. But if they do, how would they get to travel hundreds of light years through space? And if they could, why would they bother to invade us? If they're that smart, they could make everything they want for themselves using chemicals in space.

AND REMEMBER... IF ALIENS DO EXIST, THEY'D SEE YOU AS AN ALIEN, TOO!

ERK! A HIDEOUS ALIEN!

3 Meteor showers

You may be stunned to read that 20,000 tonnes of space rocks fall on Earth every year – they're mostly lumps of smashed-up asteroids. As they whizz though the air, they're called meteors and if they land they're called meteorites. But don't worry – nearly all meteors burn up before they hit the ground. The only creature ever killed by one was a dog in Egypt in 1911.

Four ways the Earth COULD be wiped out (but not for millions of years)
1 Eaten up by a black hole

In this movie, the Milky Way gets eaten by another galaxy, something that really is possible! Galaxies called (and I love this name!) cannibal galaxies actually pull other galaxies in using gravity and swallow them up. In fact, our Milky Way is a cannibal galaxy because it's currently gobbling bits of a smaller galaxy called the Sagittarius Dwarf!

As for our chances of being gobbled, there's a big galaxy called the Andromeda galaxy heading our way at 643,600 km per hour. We'll probably join it to make a bigger galaxy. Many galaxies (including the Milky Way) have black holes in their centres and when the big scrunch happens, some stars could be knocked into the black hole of either galaxy. Panicking yet? Well, DON'T… Andromeda's not due to arrive for THREE BILLION years. So there's plenty of time to finish this book and find somewhere to hide!

2 Splattered by a giant star

If a giant star blew up close to us it would be curtains. Radiation from the blast really could turn our air to nitrous oxide or laughing gas. Sounds fun, doesn't it? Trouble is, the radiation would cook us alive and boil the oceans. But don't go racing off in any rockets just yet. There are no stars near to us that are set to blow – so we're safe for hundreds of millions of years.

3 Sizzled by the Sun

The Sun's too small to blow like a giant star, but it's going to get bigger until it cooks Earth. Here's the sizzling story...

As the Sun uses up all its hydrogen gas fuel, the Sun's centre (or core) shrinks.

What's left of the Sun's core squashes together and heats up. This makes the outer parts of the Sun swell like a balloon. As the Sun grows, it cools from white-hot to red-hot. But it's still hot enough to bake us like a burned burger. The outer part of the Sun is lost into space and the core shrinks to a small glowing burned-out star called a white dwarf. Panicking yet? Don't – the big blow-out isn't due for five billion years.

4 Crushed by a comet

Comets are stony snowballs – so living on Earth is a bit like dodging a gang of snowball-chucking bullies. Except that some of the snowballs are more than 5 km across… But most comets miss us by millions of kilometres and we only get hit by a comet every half a billion years or so.

That still leaves one movie that might just possibly come true…

ASTEROID ATTACK!

Earth gets whacked by an asteroid big enough to wipe out humans every hundred million years – so that's not too often. But scientists reckon Earth's been bashed by three million asteroids of all sizes in its life. There are hits big enough to crush cities every hundred years or so. Luckily, they've missed our cities…

Luke Upwards is so impressed with the science in the *Asteroid Attack!* movie that's he's bought it from Honest Bob.

Oh well, Luke, at least you can read our space story. Just to remind you, the asteroid is heading for Earth. It's moving at twice the speed of a bullet. And it means business…

Oddblob's Alien Adventure

We tuned into an Earthling TV station to find out what the humans were doing…

I figured it would be fun to watch the blast from a distance. But the Snotties didn't like my idea.

For some reason, they thought we had to stop the asteroid. I was just about to blast it with my Blurbi-laser when Cosmo stopped me…

BLURBI-DATA

ODDBLOB, LEAVE THAT BUTTON ALONE! You'll blow the asteroid to bits but the flying bits of rock will hit Earth and do even more damage. Here are some Earthling scientists' ideas we could try...

1 Set off a bomb NEAR the asteroid to knock it off course.

2 Put a rocket on the asteroid and knock it to one side.

3 Whack it with a giant air-filled pillow (this idea was suggested by a scientist in 2002).

We didn't have bombs or rockets or giant pillows. So I thought we could sit back and enjoy the show. But Slobslime had other ideas…

For the first time in 1,000 Earth years, Slobslime had had an idea. And what's more – it actually worked!

HURRAH – THE ALIENS HAVE SAVED EARTH!

They really are space stars!

EPILOGUE: THE SKY'S THE LIMIT

And so we return to our own blue shiny Earth. OK, so I know it's a bit wet – but as far as the Solar System goes, there really is no place like home. After all, it's the only planet we humans can live on... And now you've seen what the others have to offer, maybe it's the only planet you'd *want* to live on!

Younger readers may think that space reminds them of their worst teacher. It's big and dangerous and it goes on and on for ever. But space is also beautiful and brain-boggling.

And, best of all, there's much, much more to find out. This book started with a movie and it ended with a story. But the *real-life* adventure of space is just beginning. In the future, there are sure to be millions of…

- New planets to explore.
- New stars to study.
- And perhaps even new friends to meet…?

THANKS FOR SAVING US!

HORRIBLE INDEX

Space, Stars and Slimy Aliens